KU-078-616

CONTENTS

1: STUDENT, SOLDIER

The last decade of the nineteenth century was encouraging for the parents of the future President Dwight D Eisenhower. When Ida Stover married David Eisenhower they had a ready-made home to go to – a Kansas farm given to them by David's father, who wished them to 'prosper with hard work without the savage onslaught of poverty to be overcome in their early years.' Easier ways to prosperity than farming were in David's mind after a year of this kind of work, for which he was ill-suited. His flair, he was convinced, was for commerce rather than agriculture. Possibly he had been influenced by the wide publicity given to the success of such department store proprietors as Alexander Turney Stewart in New York and William Whiteley in London. Ambitiously he sold the farm and bought a dry-goods store in the optimistically-named town of Hope in northeast Kansas. Far from having got away from farming, David Eisenhower found to his cost that his business depended exclusively on poor farmers. Drought, pestilence and negligence forced them into poverty and David into bankruptcy. He relinquished the store to his creditors and moved south to Texas, where he and his growing family found a modest house in the flourishing town of Denison, a railroad junction made prosperous by the rapidly-spreading network of the Union Pacific Railroad. There, while David was employed as a railroad worker, the Eisenhowers' third son was born on 14 October 1890. He was baptized Dwight David – Dwight because Ida Eisenhower had been told that it was the American version of the French *droit*, and straightforward, fair and upright seemed good things for any son to be.

When the new baby was two years old the family moved back to Kansas. The Eisenhowers went to Abilene, a rail and river junction which less than a quarter-century earlier had been a village accommodating the workers who had brought the Union Pacific to its terminus in the midst of endless miles of rich pasture. The village, little more than 400 acres in extent, had been settled by a pioneer called Hersey who, having made his fortune, then sold the land to a Chicago go-getter, Joe McCoy, for five dollars an acre. This was the man who was to give his name to an idiom for honesty and success, 'the real McCoy.' His idea was simply to import cattle from down-state Texas and sell it slaughtered at the railhead for five times more than he gave the cowboys who herded the longhorns a thousand miles up from the south. They in turn were well satisfied with the guaranteed price of 40 dollars a head paid them by McCoy – understandably, for the local price per head all over Edwards Plateau in southern Texas was four dollars. Thus the day of the cowboy and the industry of cattle ranching began.

The growth of Abilene – named by Mrs Hersey after the Judaean city listed by Saint Luke in his Gospel address to Theophilus – was speedy and successful. Its crooks and vandals had been driven out by the famous sheriff 'Wild Bill' Hickok and by the time the Eisenhowers got there in 1892 it was the epitome of respectability. Sixty-five years later President Eisenhower was to say to an assembly of press men that 'Abilene was so McCoy that even its newspapers told the truth – and made a profit.'

The busy town soon found a niche for the young Dwight's father as manager of the local gas plant. The directors, recommending a two-dollar increase in his weekly salary, reported him adaptable, intelligent and scrupulously fair in his treatment of employees. Similar probity was the hallmark of the Eisenhowers' family life. Wrongdoing was treated with considered punishment, but there was never any injustice. The prayer book's 'godly, righteous, and sober life' epitomized the household's routine. There was grace before meals and prayers at bedtime – 'though piety was never ponderous and rebukes for fidgeting or giggling at inappropriate moments were never harsh, since the natural exuberance of childhood was always taken into consideration.' When

Right: American machine gunners in action near Villiers-Tournelle on 20 May 1918. Some 4,355,000 US troops served in France.

THE BIOGRAPHY OF GENERAL DWIGHT D.

EISENHOWER

ALAN WYKES

3774821

973 92.0924

Published by
Bison Books Limited
17 Sherwood Place
Greenwich
Connecticut 06830, USA

© Copyright Bison Books Limited 1982

Distributed by
The Hamlyn Publishing Group Limited
London · New York · Sydney · Toronto
Astronaut House, Feltham
Middlesex, England

ISBN 0-86124-073-1

First published in 1982
All rights reserved. No part of this publication
may be reproduced, stored in a retrieval system or
transmitted in any form by any means electronic,
mechanical, photocopying or otherwise without the
permission of The Hamlyn Publishing Group
Limited and the copyright holder.

Printed in Spain

Page 1: A carefully posed shot of General
of the Army Eisenhower, taken in 1947.

Page 2–3: Eisenhower, Watson and
Montgomery are photographed during a
visit to Third Armored Division in
Wiltshire on 25 February 1944.

Page 4–5: Landing Ship Tanks landing
supplies on Omaha Beach after the initial
assault.

Above: Cadet Dwight David Eisenhower in 1915, the year he graduated from West Point Military Academy.

a child herself, Ida Stover had memorized considerable stretches of the Bible and could usually produce an appropriate reproach in the language of the prophets and apostles. 'Why stand ye idle all day?,' she would enquire of any of her six sons discovered evading a duty; and to any of them grubby from boisterous romping, 'And he took him a potsherd to scrape himself withal.'

The tall, narrow frame house on the corner of the Abilene street had a high gable giving it something of the look of a cadaver wearing a steeple hat; but although piety, frugality and industry were important facets of the family's life, Dwight never heard an exchange of anger between his parents, and his own amiable character was rarely at odds with those of his brothers. 'They fought,' Ida reminisced to a reporter when she was 80 years old, 'but only in good humor.' She had by then joined the Jehovah's Witnesses and there were many snide newspaper comments about the irony of a pacifist being the mother of a general. Eisenhower's conventional reply was that he hated war only marginally less than he hated the Nazis.

It was, then, in a cheerful environment that the future Supreme Commander, President and folk hero spent his formative years. There were regular domestic chores to be undertaken and frequent reference to the axiom that God helps those who help themselves. Delusions of grandeur were laughed off, self-respect and self-discipline were lauded as the greatest virtues; no man was better than another save by his efforts and achievements; and in a land dedicated to individual opportunity it was natural that the prevailing national sentiment should be that of Stephen Decatur: 'My country, right or wrong!' In 1943 Dwight Eisenhower was to remind his younger brother Milton, who had just been inaugurated into the presidency of Kansas State College, of one of the responsibilities of the educator: 'It is the necessity of teaching and inculcating good, old-fashioned patriotism.'

That chauvinistic sentiment was highly popular in the Western World in the early years of the twentieth century. The United States, glowing with the brash pride of independence conclusively won at Yorktown scarcely more than a century earlier, revelled in the manifestation of that pride in the naval and military colleges of Annapolis and West Point. Annapolis had an entrance system restricted by the number of representatives in Congress, two cadets being admitted annually for each senator and delegate, but West Point had no such restriction. Only the accommodation limit of 2496 cadets halted entry. The Eisenhower boys having been left free to choose their own paths in life, Dwight opted for the army and at the age of 21 entered West Point Military Academy.

Eisenhower's record at the Abilene high school had not been an impressive one, but he was no idler. He was strongest in history, applied mathematics, art (like Churchill he became an amateur painter of some ability) and sport. One of his teachers was to remark that 'at times he was slow in comprehension to the point of denseness,' but that was because his reasoning was never glib and he would walk round a problem rather than approach it direct, thus seeing it from several viewpoints. This characteristic was to develop into his grasp of the art of diplomacy – 'Not that any such highfalutin concept entered my head; I just saw the advantage of being tactful. Maybe because antagonizing people never seemed to me a good way of getting on with them.' His widespread popularity was established at an early date.

His brother Arthur recalled an incident in Abilene in 1896, when Dwight was six. 'That was presidential campaign year for William McKinley and William Jennings Bryan and there was a torchlight march through the town starting out from the theater we used to call the Op'ry House and ending at the mayor's office. Our parents were strong for the Republican ticket and McKinley had the backing of Marcus Hanna and other big industrialists in an election fought mainly over high protective tariffs. Feelings ran as high as the McKinley tariffs and demonstrations in

Congress were reflected in the spirit of the people.

'So off we all started, carrying improvised torches which were wads of waste soaked in oil and pierced by mother's hatpins fixed to the ends of long sticks. We Eisenhowers were somewhere in the middle of the column, and Dwight, the smallest, was in the middle of us – dad, my other brother and me. When we passed our house mom was there at the window holding the baby and waving and Dwight wriggled out of the column and dashed to the rear so

that he could pass mom again and wave back. It was a spontaneous gesture of affection that earned him a shoulder-high ride for the rest of the march. Symbolic in a way.'

The schoolboy had as many buddies as he liked to talk – and listen – to; and he mixed easily with girls and boys alike. 'He had the gift of making you feel you were more important than he was himself,' said Omar Bradley, his classmate at West Point. 'Blood-and-guts' Patton ('our blood, his guts' was the GI comment), whose opposite Eisen-

hower was, interpreted the gift as 'no more than pushing out a cover-up for his mighty inferiority complex.' From a different viewpoint Patton, with his spectacular flamboyance and contempt for human emotions, could have been accused of a similar propped-up weakness. Whatever Eisenhower's subconscious reasoning, there can be no doubt about his Carnegian ability to win

Below: Eisenhower's class at West Point. Eisenhower was a conscientious and popular but undistinguished student.

New York American

LUSITANIA DEAD 1,256---115 AMERICANS
GERMANY OFFICIALLY ADMITS SINKING SHIP

U. S. WILL ACT QUICKLY: DRASTIC STEPS URGED AS INDIGNATION RISES

Wilson Besieged with Telegrams and Situation Is Regarded as Most Momentous in Many Years—Gerard Cabled for Germany's Explanation

Washington, May 8.—The rising tide of popular indignation against the sinking of the Lusitania by a German submarine with the consequent enormous loss of life of American citizens has caused Administration officials to indicate more positive views for comprehensive action than was revealed by those officials earlier in day.

The apparent effort of these officials, struggling with injunctions of secrecy, is to produce the impression, although not in the form of official statement, that early and decided action is to be expected from the Administration in answer to a popular demand. High officials to-night indicated their belief that action will be forced although they would make no prediction as to the precise

HUNDREDS MASSED ON DECK AS LINER REARED IN HER DEATH PLUNGE

Survivors Tell Thrilling Stories of Last Fateful Moments—Sixty Perish as Lifeboat Falls—Mothers Clasping Dead Babies Picked Up in Water

Special Cable to International News Service.
Queenstown, May 8.—Thrilling stories of the Lusitania disaster were told by survivors who landed here. F. J. Gauntlett, of New York, traveling in company with A. L. Hopkins, president of the Newport News Shipbuilding Co. (who is missing), and S. M. Knox, president of the New York Shipbuilding Co., Philadelphia—listed as saved), said:

"I was lingering in the dining saloon chatting with friends when the first explosion occurred. We knew at once what had happened. Shortly afterward the ship listed perceptibly. I shouted to the others to close the ports. Some of us then went to our staterooms and put on life belts. Going on deck we were

GERMANY'S OFFICIAL STATEMENT

Berlin, Via Wireless to London, May 9, 2:45 A. M.
THE following official communication was issued to-night:

"The Cunard liner Lusitania was yesterday torpedoed by a German submarine and sank.

"The Lusitania was naturally armed with guns, as were recently most of the English mercantile steamers. Moreover, as is well known here, she had large quantities of war material in her cargo.

"Her owners, therefore, knew to what danger the passengers were exposed. They alone bear all the responsibility for what has happened.

"Germany, on her part, left nothing undone to repeatedly and strongly warn them. The Imperial Ambassador in Washington even went so far as to make a public warning, so as to draw attention to this danger. The English press sneered then at the warning and relied on the protection of the British fleet to safeguard Atlantic traffic."

Geneva, May 8.—A dispatch from Munich, Bavaria, says the German Submarine U 39 sank the Lusitania. There were great rejoicings during to-day in Southern Germany.

FROHMAN'S BODY IS FOUND; VANDERBILT AND HUBBARD LOST

London, May 8.—The first list of identified dead in the Lusitania disaster was given out here this afternoon. The bodies of the following persons have been recovered and positively identified, and are being embalmed:

DR. F. S. PEARSON, of New York.
MRS. AMELIA McDONALD.
PATRICK CALLON.
ARTHUR FOLEY.
Other identified Americans dead are:
MRS. MAY BROWN.
CHARLES PLAMONDON.
J. FELLMAN or FILLMAN.
P. L. JONES.

Above: The sinking of the *Lusitania* and the loss of 128 American lives hardened America's attitude to entering the war.

friends and influence people. He was not a natural leader in the sense of having a dominating power of command, as had Patton; rather, he took others with him through his understanding of their problems. Only in games did an element of ruthlessness show itself. He played fast, tough football and baseball at high school and as a spectator was an equally efficient cheerleader. 'He could out-shout the lot of us,' Arthur said in a letter to Jim Hagerty, Eisenhower's PR man during the 1952 presidential campaign, 'and there's no doubt he will do so again if required.'

Far from shouting, he was awestruck when on the day of his entry into West Point he was required to take the oath of allegiance: 'I pledge allegiance to the flag of the United States of America and to the Republic for which it stands – one nation, indivisible, with liberty and justice for all.' 'A feeling came over me,' he wrote in his autobiographical *At Ease*, 'that the expression "The United States of America" would now and henceforth mean something different than it ever had before. From here it would be the nation I was serving, not

myself. Suddenly the flag itself meant something. I haven't heard other officers speak of their memories of that moment but mine have never left me. Across half a century I can look back and see a rawboned, gawky Kansas boy from farm country, earnestly repeating the words that would make him a cadet.'

As a cadet he rubbed shoulders not only with Omar Bradley but also with Mark Clark. Both were to be under his command in the Allies' conquest of Nazi Germany; but they have both said in their memoirs that at West Point they detected no special signs of brilliance in him. 'He was out on the football field or hoking up a poker or bridge game more often than he was studying; but study time was study time, and when he was in class he was all concentration . . . In the ballistics tutorial he worked out a complicated calculus problem in his own way and more than once his methods were seen to be better than the laid-down ones and used in place of them.'

Such flukes aside, Eisenhower eased his way through West Point without distinction, save in sports – though

unfortunately he had to give up active participation on the field because of a leg injury sustained in a baseball game. However local baseball teams found him well worth a dollar an hour as a coach and three dollars a game as a cheerleader. Poker and bridge were his other sources of supplementary income. His aptitude for cards saw him over many a financial hiatus, for he could milk even a poor hand of its full worth; while as a good loser he was never short of gaming companions. His humor was as widespread as the ear-to-ear grin that was to become world famous, a gift to caricaturists, but humor for Eisenhower meant clowning rather than subtlety. His way of deflating the pomposity of a cadet using the brief authority of a temporary corporal's rank to order Eisenhower to appear before him in full dress coat, was to appear in full dress coat and nothing else. Throughout his life he was to enjoy simple-minded jokes and custard-pie comedy and it was perhaps such basic humor as much as anything else that added to his endearing qualities. Even his father, reproaching him for his frequent attendance at poolrooms and barn dances, could not dispute the logic of Dwight's assertion that 'recreation is the other side of the coin of work.'

While Eisenhower was plodding and playing through the curriculum at West Point, Europe was heading toward the holocaust sparked off by the assassination in Sarajevo on 28 June 1914 of the Archduke Francis Ferdinand and his wife. Yet when Britain declared war on Germany on 4 August the United States rallied round the cherished Jeffersonian idea of independence – 'Entangling alliances with none' – as if America was wholly detached from any civilization east of the Atlantic. The United States touching faith in the assurance of David Starr Jordan's World Peace Foundation that 'Humanly speaking [war] is impossible' received scarcely a jolt when Germany invaded Belgium, and President Wilson's proclamation of neutrality seemed to establish for all time their complete detachment from the affairs of the Old World. Seemingly it had not occurred to them that the ancestry of most Americans was European, that racial links are hard to break, and that memories of injustices, real or imagined, are persistant. There were German Americans who had inherited a hatred for British empire-building, Irish-Americans who had never forgotten Cromwell and American Jews who were embittered by the anti-Semitism displayed by Russia (the third signatory of the Triple Entente). There was also great sympathy with France who had been foremost with help in the American Revolution and Belgium, disgracefully trampled over despite her neutrality. Whatever Wilson might declare about keeping out of European affairs he could not change people's antagonisms and sympathies. Although American money and American goods were fully available to both the Allies and the Central Powers, it was impossible for Congress to ignore the overwhelming antipathy to Germany when intensification of the U-Boat war resulted in the loss of 128 American lives in the *Lusitania*, torpedoed by the submarine *U-20* off the Irish coast on 7 May 1915.

Two months later Eisenhower graduated from West Point with the rank of second lieutenant and was immediately posted to the 19th Infantry Regiment at Fort San Antonio, Texas. He had been there only two days when he met a girl from Denver, Colorado, who was visiting a friend of her family, a major on the staff. Her name was Mamie Geneva Doud. At the camp the talk was all of the need, now, to snap out of the policy of isolation; but Eisenhower was too smitten with Mamie's attractions – she was both good-looking and lively – to absorb or express opinions on mere political maneuvers. 'I was balled over,' he wrote to his younger brother Milton (then in his freshman year at Kansas State University): 'what a pitcher she is!' He courted Mamie for a year and in July 1916 married her.

By that time the climate of isolationism had cooled considerably. Much of it had sunk below the Atlantic with the *Lusitania*, and although there were many of the pro-German persuasion who muttered that she had been carrying arms (as indeed she had) and was not therefore entitled to the protection of the neutrality laws, there were too many Americans killed or injured in that and subsequent attacks by German U-Boats for the much louder anti-German mutterings to be subdued. Wilson made an abrupt U-turn in the early part of 1916 and in his presidential defense-program speech he crudely adapted Chorus's lines from *Henry V* and announced that 'All the rest of the world is on fire, and our own house is not fireproof.' On 3 June he signed the National Defense Act and celebrated it in Washington by

Below: Eisenhower courted Mamie Geneva for a bare year before marrying her in July 1916.

leading a procession down Pennsylvania Avenue.

The Act provided for an increase in the strength of the army to a maximum of 220,000 and the spending of $313,000,000 on new warships. 'It's a paradox,' Eisenhower wrote to Mamie after the reelection of Wilson to the White House at the end of 1916, 'that he got back to Washington on the strength of the slogan "He kept us out of the war" and we're now in it, or damn near. And I guess I may well be on the first draft, which apart from leaving you I'd welcome. These Huns have got to be given a showdown.' He was not on the first or any other draft. The commanding officer at San Antonio recommended his transfer in the rank of captain to a new regiment of conscripts, the 57th Infantry, as an instructor, 'in which capacity he shows particular merits,' and on the day America entered the war, 6 April 1917, he was posted.

It was June before the first contingents of American troops arrived in France with their commander in chief Major General John Pershing. By that time Eisenhower had proved himself indispensable as a company officer and instructor in the handling of weapons and vehicles. 'Trapped in his own talents,' said his brother Arthur, 'he fretted to be at the front with the illustrious Pershing; only Mamie's pregnancy offered him any consolation for what he thought might be seen as draft-dodging. It had to be hammered into him time after time that allegiance to the flag took many forms.'

The Eisenhowers' first son was born on 24 September, while Dwight was on posting to the staff of the Officer Training Unit at Fort Oglethorpe, Georgia. His elation was intensified by the promise of promotion to the rank of major and appointment to his first command – of the Tank Corps training school at Camp Colt, Gettysburg. 'Promotion and progeny in a single week,' he wrote to his parents. 'Howzzat?' It was the impish query of a schoolboy scoring the winning point for his team, devoid of any conceit, but his mother had a ready tag in reply: 'We are thankful, your Dad and I, for you and Mamie, but do not forget the Book says "I know thy pride and the naughtiness of thy heart," so be thankful to God but "boast not thyself of tomorrow; for thou knowest

not what a day may bring forth".' It was ironic that Eisenhower, a non-boaster if ever there was one, should lose his first-born in a scarlet-fever epidemic in 1921. His promotion however was ratified, and after a brief spell with the 65th Engineer Regiment he helped with its reorganization into the Tank Corps and in March 1918 took command at Camp Colt.

By that time the tank had become a force to be reckoned with in battle. The trench system of warfare demanded an offensive weapon that could surmount parapets, cross ditches, crush barbed wire and take firepower close to the enemy lines in support of infantry. The 'land battleships' developed from the 'crawler' tractors marketed for agricultural use by the Holt Manufacturing Company of California in 1906 appeared to fill this need, but their development was slow, opposed by traditionalists, and hindered by manufacturing difficulties. Deceptive names such as 'Little Willie,' 'Centipede,' 'Mother' and finally Tank were devised to screen the real purpose of the ungainly monsters from the enemy. After much trouble the 28-ton Mark I AAV (Armored Assault Vehicle) with its crew of eight, two six-pounder guns, four machine guns and lumbering speed of under four miles an hour, saw action at the tail end of the Battle of the Somme on 15 September 1916. Its real value was not seen until it was used in large numbers at Cambrai on 20 November 1917. Nearly 400 Mark IV tanks

supported by infantry, artillery and aircraft smashed through the Hindenburg Line on a wide front and, but for bad planning in the upper echelons of command, would have avoided the German counterattack that reversed the British triumph. There was no doubt that with the arrival on the battlefield of this armor-plated sluggard with its sweating crew and monstrous appearance a new concept of warfare had become a reality. Rather oddly, the Germans treated the tank contemptuously. Perhaps they were deceived by the ease with which they had turned the tables at Cambrai.

If the Germans were deceived the English, French and Americans certainly were not. The leading campaigner for armored formations was Colonel JFC Fuller, whose theories eventually permeated the thinking of all the Allies' High Commands and through them down to the training establishments. At Camp Colt, Eisenhower, now a temporary Lieutenant Colonel, deputized for the Washington-based commanding officer to the extent of running the show entirely, from the training of the intake to the dispatch of crews and tanks overseas. However a month after his promotion the war ended and so did Eisenhower's colonelcy.

'For a few days I faltered in my

Below: Eisenhower trained tank crews at Camp Colt and dispatched them for duty on the Western Front.

dedication to the idea of service in uniform. Couldn't I serve the nation just as well in cits? I'd had an offer from a business man and I could have walked into a hundred bucks a week more than I was ever likely to get in the army. There was no war to fight and I felt disheartened.'

Evidently he did not feel downhearted for long. As soon as officers who had fought in Europe began to return, Eisenhower's enthusiasm was renewed – in particular by Colonel George Patton, an officer who, though poles apart from Eisenhower in character and later to be extremely critical of him, was of like mind regarding armored warfare. Both men held the view that tanks should be used as spearheads as well as in support of infantry and that advances in design

should be called for so that the machine was fast as well as destructive. The establishment regarded the tank as a sort of lumbering gun-carriage that was better protected but less maneuverable than one drawn by a team of horses. Since both Eisenhower and Patton published their radical views in official army journals, they were rapped over the knuckles by higher authority and told to curb their enthusiasm for the maverick war engine. In the event it made little difference, for the Tank Corps, always a suspect formation in the eyes of cavalrymen, was reembodied in the infantry from which it had sprung and Eisenhower and Patton henceforth followed different paths.

Eisenhower's took him to Panama, where the caretaking force in the Canal

Above: A US Renault FT-17 light tank with the driver's hatch open on the Western Front in 1918.

Zone was commanded by Pershing's late principal staff officer, Brigadier General Fox Connor. Connor had heard of Eisenhower's clash with authority over the role of the tank and had decided that here was the untrammelled thinker he would welcome as a trainee in the wider reaches of staff work. For three years, from 1922–25, Connor was Eisenhower's mentor. It is difficult to imagine a better one. Steeped in the military history of all ages, Connor shared his knowledge with a diligent pupil who later was to write, 'In my three years with Connor at Camp Gaillard I learnt more about the war game than they'd stuffed into me in all my time at West Point. At the Point it was almost exclusively the Civil War – as if there had never been another war from which one could learn something about tactics and intentions.'

Below: Tanks of 10th Battalion, 37th Division pass infantry and captured 4.2-inch guns.

From Panama Eisenhower went to the Staff College at Fort Leavenworth, Kansas, from which he graduated with honors in June 1926 and spent six weeks accumulated leave with Mamie and their second son, John, who had been born in 1922. He wrote to Leroy Watson, an old classmate at West Point that his name had 'come out of the hat' for advancement to the highest echelon

of command, the War Department. His assignments there were of no more than routine interest – they included writing an official summary of actions involving the American Expeditionary Force in the war, and a year's posting on the Battle Monuments Commission in Paris – but their great value was that they took him into the company of the two most influential men in the War Depart-

ment at that time: Chief of Staff General Pershing, and Colonel George Marshall, Pershing's aide.

Marshall, a taciturn man, saw the value to the army of Eisenhower's natural bonhomie and his talents as a tactician and organizer. As a first step to the full exploitation of those talents he recommended him for a further course of advanced studies, this time at the War College, Washington, where Connor was now Commandant. Reports of his brilliance there filtered through to Marshall, who earmarked him for appointment to the Executive Office of the Assistant Secretary of War, Major General Moseley.

Moseley had a job ready-made for him: to investigate the possibilities of industrial cooperation with the War Department. Such possibilities were few and far between. Industry was still living on the fat of its heyday of war profiteering and sensed that cooperation was a euphemism for price control, which indeed it was. Also, if the League of Nations were determined to end war there would be no need for cooperation with the War Department. Thus ran the premise, but with a troubled and re-

calcitrant Germany unable to cope with the impossible reparations demanded by the Versailles Treaty, it was fairly obvious to the War Department that at the very least some tentative plans for preparation might be laid down. When such intentions became known there sprang into existence a hydra-headed opposition: the World Peace Foundation, the War Resisters International, the Committee on the Cause and Cure of War, the American League Against War and the National Council for the Pre-vention of War – the heads were impressively named, but all concealed varying degrees of continuing attachment to the Jeffersonian principle of 'entangling alliances with none.' Yet as the financier Bernard Baruch reminded Eisenhower, 'Ethics is one thing, profits another.' Baruch had been head of the War Industries Board, owned the Baltimore & Ohio Railroad, and was highly informed on fiscal matters. 'You will find them co-operative if you talk in terms of orders.'

Eisenhower did just that. His second spell with Connor had shown him that the development of the tank and the aircraft was leading to the full mechanization of warfare. So with the vehement approval of the newly-appointed Chief of Staff, General Douglas MacArthur, Eisenhower canvassed the tycoons of industry and won them over to the War Department's side. It says much for his diplomacy that even the United States Steel Corporation, which was inextricably knotted into the Carnegie Endow-

ment for International Peace, cooperated in his plan for the mobilization of industry in the event of war. This plan resulted among other things in the founding of the Industrial College, an offshoot of the War College devoted entirely to the study of industry's meth-

Right: Eisenhower's year with the Battle Monuments Commission brought him into contact with Pershing and Marshall.

Below: Men of the 5th Canadian Mounted Rifles exercising with a Mark IV tank. Eisenhower early recognized the future importance of the tank.

Left: Eisenhower is to the left of MacArthur as he is formally welcomed to Manila by the 31st Infantry.

ods and problems.

Industry had problems of greater magnitude and of more immediate concern than cooperation with the army, though their willingness was noted with approval. The 1920s had brought chain stores, moving assembly lines for the mass production of every commodity from automobiles to cigarette lighters, a proliferation of skyscrapers and great conurbations, synthetic materials, Hollywood, refrigeration and ice cream for everyone, advertising and public relations, hire purchase and dreams of wealth beyond dreams. In October 1929 the dream turned to nightmare with the Wall Street crash and the Depression.

The war veterans who had been promised bonus payments for their service and who had been fobbed off with insurance policies that the government refused to honor at their face value demonstrated their anger on the steps of the Capitol. Ordered by President Hoover to deal with the demonstrators in military manner, MacArthur fed them from mobile kitchens, put them under canvas at Anacostia Flats nearby and allowed them squatters' rights in empty tenements in Pennsylvania Avenue. Inevitably, the numbers were swelled by nonveterans who were nonetheless hungry and homeless. Police attempts at eviction led to disorder and shooting and the Secretary for War ordered MacArthur to 'use troops, not kid gloves.' Tanks, infantry and cavalry were summoned and Eisenhower and Patton accompanied MacArthur to the Flats and dispersed the marchers with tear gas and a show of force.

The event gave Eisenhower his first sight of the workings of a combination of economics and politics that was, and was always to remain, mystifying to him. 'I can understand a man's problems,' he wrote to Mamie, 'but the deviousness of these politicians is beyond me. For instance, how can anyone in the White House get mixed up in corruption as Harding did?' (Warren Harding, President from 1921–23, had surrounded himself with sycophants and crooks who fiddled the public treasury, accepted bribes and stole the money that should have been accumulating to back the insurance policies the Bonus Marchers had come to Washington to claim.) The answer was, of course, that the higher the office the easier the mechanics of corruption. Eisenhower's naiveté was to reveal itself again when, during his presidential term, he appointed Richard M Nixon as his vice-president.

A change of heart on the part of the American electorate brought Roosevelt the Democrat to the White House in 1933. His New Deal to restore prosperity involved a cut of $80,000,000 in military expenditure, which could hardly be expected to raise cheers from the Chief of Staff. Nor did it. MacArthur, viewing with a professional eye the threat to peace smoldering in the rearmament of Germany and Japan, told the President that the cut in expenditure was tantamount to betrayal of the American people. For the head of the army to imply that the President is a traitor, even in justifiable anger, itself approaches *lèse-majesté*; it says much for Roosevelt's self-control that he accepted MacArthur's apology but merely told him not to be a fool when he contritely offered his resignation. Clearly though the two men were politically and emotionally abrasive and Roosevelt solved the problem by sending MacArthur to the Philippines to organize the islands' defenses for President Manuel Quezon. This was by no means the casting into outer darkness it seemed to MacArthur's many sympathizers; in fact the appointment had considerable significance for him. His father, Brigadier General Arthur MacArthur had been Governor General in 1901 and Douglas himself had served in the American occupation force after graduating from West Point in 1903. 'It was crystal clear to me,' he wrote in his memoirs, 'that the future and, indeed, the very existence of America, were irrevocably entwined with . . . its island outposts.'

When he went to the Philippines in 1935 he took Eisenhower with him as his adjutant. Eisenhower had lost his lieutenant colonelcy after the war and substantively he was still only a captain, but MacArthur immediately promoted him to major and in 1936 restored to him his full substantive rank of lieutenant colonel. 'I pop up and down like a jack-in-the-box,' he wrote to Mamie, but from then on there were no demotions; he was on the way up.

2: STRATEGIST

Eisenhower was with General MacArthur in the Philippines for four years. The regard the General had for his adjutant was not wholeheartedly returned. MacArthur tended to abandon responsibilities in small matters if it suited him and when the comeback hit his staff he turned their resentment aside with disdain. Such an attitude was completely out of key with Eisenhower's concern for the men who worked with him. But if his regard for MacArthur as a man was something less than his appreciation of his brilliance as a general, there was no showdown and the overall strategic and political experience gained was of great value to him.

When, as a result of Britain's foolish and muddled policies *vis-à-vis* Germany, Hitler marched his forces into Poland on 1 September 1939, Eisenhower immediately went to MacArthur and asked to be returned to Washington 'ready for action.' MacArthur's reply was that any action affecting the United States would be 'right here in the Philippines' and indeed the islands had been under continual threat of invasion since the aggressive expansionist policy of the Japanese had first taken shape in 1931.

Eisenhower persisted and MacArthur's reluctance to lose his right-hand man was eventually worn down. Eisenhower was home for Christmas and in January 1940 was given the task of organizing full-scale army maneuvers in California. The exercise, involving all available troops and the National Guard was a great success and brought Eisenhower again into the view of Marshall, Patton and Leonard Gerow, head of the War Department's War Plans Division, who had been Eisenhower's fellow student at Fort Leavenworth. The commander of the United States Third Army, General Walter Kreuger, was summoned to Washington to be told by Marshall, who was now Chief of Staff, that Eisenhower was 'gifted beyond the ordinary with abilities worth watching' – a sentence that could almost be counted as a speech from the taciturn Marshall. Kreuger duly watched.

Patton and Gerow too were watching. Patton, remembering Eisenhower's radical views on tanks, wanted him in the expanding armored force; Gerow saw him as a brilliant strategist, ideal as a member of the War Plans Division. In the event he was given command of an infantry regiment for five months and then, as he told Mamie with irritation, was 'hauled up the ladder to another Staff job.' It irked him to think that with the United States on the brink of inevitable war he might repeat his experience of the earlier conflict and never see action. It pleased him that his appointment was as Chief of Staff to General Kreuger, for the Third Army was a widely scattered mass of untrained troops into whom he had to inculcate the impetus of unity. 'Most of all,' he had written, 'morale is promoted by unity – unity in service to the country and in determination to attain the objective of national security.'

Left: Eisenhower spent four profitable years in the Philippines with Douglas MacArthur.

Right: Japanese troops impassively watch Manila burn as they approach for a beach landing.

National security had been inextricably tied up with the new National Defense Act of 1920, which limited the strength of the army to 280,000 – of which only 135,000 had actually been enlisted. Isolationism was a powerful force based on the misguided belief that if a great nation outlawed war, war would cease to exist. This spurious notion was nourished by quasi-Fascist organizations such as the Silver Shirt Legion, the National Party, the Liberty Party and the Ku Klux Klan. Roosevelt's administration was afflicted by many such isolationists and fellow travellers including, among the Republican opposition, the anglophobe Gerald Nye. Nye was a Congressman from North Dakota, who chaired a Senate committee investigating the wickedness of an economy based on the profits of armaments manufacture. When Nye had dealt with this king-size sin he turned

Below: Despite the massive growth of support for Nazism, in 1934 the United States was still isolationist.

Right: Colonel Eisenhower in 1940 was given the task of promoting Third Army morale and hardening the troops.

to such subtle evils as the British 'mania' for making anti-Nazi films and thereby encouraging a European decadence which threatened America's innocent hands. Congress took care to preserve that innocence by forcing Roosevelt to approve, in 1935, legislation to ensure neutrality.

During 1935 Hitler noisily defied the Versailles Treaty by commanding compulsory military service and the formation of the Luftwaffe; Mussolini invaded Abyssinia; and the Fascist *Croix de Feu* was founded in France. A few months later Franco was appointed dictator by the insurgents in the Spanish Civil War; in the Far East Chiang Kai-shek opened a united front against Japan; and in London Oswald Mosley's anti-Semitic Blackshirts marched on Whitechapel, the Jewish quarter. Neutrality was equated with superiority and Congress forbade the supply of food,

money, ships, arms, oil or munitions to any belligerent country. Also Americans were forbidden to travel in the ships of any nation that had raised a hand against another. It was a time of fear, uncertainty and prejudice.

Regardless of the alarmist outpourings from the isolationists Roosevelt and Marshall had kept going within the War Department the all-important War Plans Division, headed in 1940 by Gerow. The Division had for nearly 20 years been making and remaking plans for dealing with every conceivable enemy, including Great Britain. However their plans naturally demanded money to be spent on ships and armies and the mere $1,000,000,000 allotted to armaments in 1936 had to be disguised as unemployment alleviation. Even that was seen by the critics as warmongering and soon after China confronted Japan Roosevelt had to issue an apologetic warning: 'Let no one imagine that America will escape, that America may expect mercy, that this Western Hemisphere will not be attacked.' The declaration of war by Britain and France on Germany on 3 September 1939 brought the less force-ful isolationists to a different way of thinking. On 4 November the President signed a new act repealing the Neutrality Bill to the extent of allowing the sale of arms on a cash-and-carry basis to belligerent nations who were not thought to be a threat to the United States – by implication Britain and France.

Eisenhower was thus less hindered in his job of promoting the morale of the Third Army than the continuance of full neutrality would have allowed. Only with the surrender of Finland to Russia, and of Holland, Belgium and France to Germany – all between 12 March and 25 June 1940 – did America take to panic stations and vote seven billion dollars for naval, air, and land forces. Yet although the President might say 'We will extend to the opponents of force the material resources of this nation,' he also had to hint at the forth-

Above: Brigadier General Eisenhower discusses plans with Gerow and Crawford in 1942.

coming compulsory military service, for arms and machines were of little use without the men to use them. Such was the speed of events in Europe that barely a year passed before it became clear that with the stranglehold of the Luftwaffe tightening on Britain and the battle of the Atlantic raging there might soon be a threat of attack by the German navy along the United States' eastern seaboard. The hint at conscription became a demand and, despite the isolationists' weakening but still persistent protests, popularly voiced by the folk hero Colonel Charles Lindbergh ('We believe that the security of our country lies in the strength and character of our people, and not in fighting foreign wars') the bill calling up the first million men

Left: Eisenhower, Chief of Staff to Third Army, with General Walter Kreuger in 1941.

for a maximum of one year's service was passed in the autumn of 1940. Roosevelt had to sugar the pill with his famous promise to American mothers: 'I shall say it again and again and again – your boys are not going to be sent into any foreign wars.' Yet in another of his 'fireside chats' over the radio he shrewdly added: 'If Britain should go down all of us in the Americas would be living at the point of a gun, a gun loaded with explosive bullets, economic as well as military.' Like most politicians he liked to ensure that he could fall back on the useful phrase 'I told you so' if necessary.

Below: Eisenhower discusses procedure with James Bradley, Deputy Chief of Staff, Fourth Army.

Eisenhower's service with the Third Army was interrupted on 12 December 1941 by a message summoning him to Washington for emergency duty. The emergency was the Japanese attack on Pearl Harbor five days earlier. The announcement on the radio had fallen with shattering impact into the somnolence of an extraordinarily summery Sunday afternoon. The journalist Alistair Cooke wrote that 'Sunday afternoons in winter were an American institution: the New York Philharmonic piped from coast to coast its regular concert over the only mass medium we had, the radio. My Washington host, an official of the British Supply Council, easily persuaded me to settle in his living room as the orchestra started to tune up, and the strings and woodwinds went skittering up and down the scale. It was about to launch into a Shostakovich symphony when there was an

abrupt halt and a crackle on the radio. A breathless voice said, "One moment, please," and then: "The Japanese have attacked Pearl Harbor, the United States naval base on Oahu Island in the Hawaiian Islands." The designation of "Oahu Island" instead of "Honolulu" was a small recognition of our vague sense, in those far-off days, of Pacific geography. I suspect that not one American in a hundred, on that brilliant day, knew that Honolulu was the main base of the American Pacific fleet.'

Eisenhower, never averse to snatching a few hours' sleep, had gone to bed that afternoon to enable him 'to tackle the next day's work with vigor,' and told his aide that in no circumstances was he to be awakened. Pearl Harbor too was asleep. Antiaircraft guns were unmanned, ships were unprotected by torpedo nets and an excessive number of the fleet's regular complement was on leave.

Also it chanced that that weekend a draft of conscripted men had been released and were on their way home after serving the mandatory year with the forces. All told, one might say, a weekend of idyllic peace. Ironically a Japanese declaration of war and a 'red alert' from the United States Chief of Naval Operations, Admiral Harold Stark, were somewhere in the pipeline of communications, but for reasons which have never been satisfactorily explained, were delayed. In any case, the Commander in Chief of the United States fleet, Admiral Husband E Kimmel, seems to have been in a state of complacent torpor. The crippling within two hours of virtually the entire Pacific Fleet's battle force by dive bombers and torpedo bombers aroused him in time to face his dismissal, charitably disguised as retirement, five days later. Yet as Eisenhower recorded, 'The sinking or damaging of eighteen warships and nearly two hundred airplanes, plus the killing and wounding of over two thousand men of the Navy and Marine Corps could not be considered as anything but a justification for a declaration of war, so in a way Kimmel the scapegoat can be seen as bringing about the ultimate defeat of the Japanese, for Yamamoto himself [the architect of the Pearl Harbor attack] forecast that our full fury would be unleashed as a consequence of the "Day of Infamy." '

Left: A Mitsubishi A6M Zero takes off for the Pearl attack, which brought America to war.

Below: The Mitsubishi Ki-21 Sally was one of the Japanese Army Air Force's chief bombers at the start of the Pacific War.

As indeed it was. Every faction in America was immediately united in outrage. Congress next day voted with one accord to declare war on Japan. (To be strictly accurate, there was one vote against the proposition – that of a female pacifist in the House of Representatives who had held out in 1917 too. 'Over my dead body,' she shouted, and left the House to the accompaniment of a few ironic cheers.) On 11 December Germany and Italy, in response to Congress's outraged anger, declared war on the United States; and it was thus to the drums of all-out war that Eisenhower was summoned to Washington on 12 December.

Not unnaturally he supposed that the 'emergency duty' would be service in the field. His son John, then in his first year at West Point, has said that his father's heart was 'leaping at the thought of a scrap at last.' If it was, it was soon to be calmed. General Marshall had decided that yet another desk job was to replace Eisenhower's activities at Third Army.

'I know,' said Marshall, 'that you were recommended by one General for division command and by another for corps command. That's all very well. I'm glad they have that opinion of you, but you're going to stay right here and fill your position, and that's that.' It was a heavy blow. 'The frustration I had felt in 1918 because of my failure to get overseas now returned briefly. By General Marshall's word I was completely condemned to a desk job in Washington for the duration.' However, he replied manfully, 'General, I came into this office to do my duty. If that locks me to a desk for the rest of the war, so be it!' Saluting formally, the absurdity of this line of dialogue suddenly struck him. He turned, grinning through the stiff upper lip, and saw that 'a tiny smile quirked the corner of [Marshall's] face.'

This was an achievement indeed, Marshall's smiles were extremely rare. So was his praise. He took the hard line that efficiency was its own reward. If anyone failed or looked like failing in a task, replacement was immediate; but his assessments of capabilities were so careful that firings were fewer than hirings. His choice of Eisenhower to

suggest a course of action regarding the Philippines, where MacArthur was still in command and which were now threatened with Japanese invasion, was based firmly on Eisenhower's experience there as MacArthur's Chief of Staff plus a reputation gained for willingness to accept responsibility. It was the willingness to accept responsibility that was of paramount importance. 'Eisenhower,' Marshall said, 'the Department is filled with able men who analyze their problems well but feel compelled to bring them to me for final solution. I must have assistants who will solve their own problems and tell me later what they have done.'

As a test Marshall asked Eisenhower to produce a plan of action for the Philippines. The plan was typed by Eisenhower himself on a single sheet of yellow copy paper. It pointed out that despite the threat to the islands and the inability of the Pacific Fleet, battered into impotence at Pearl Harbor, to make any effective display of force, it was nonetheless important to prevent both Filipino and American forces from feeling that they had been abandoned. The recommended actions were few and tersely set down. They amounted to building up a base of operations in Australia from which supplies and personnel could be moved into the Philippines, sending army pursuit planes from San Diego to Australia either by aircraft carrier or by the fastest available commercial vessel, ferrying the planes from Australia to the Philippines and influencing Russia to enter the war so that Japanese troops were diverted to Manchuria and air bases made available to

American bombers to strike at Japan.

The plan fitted perfectly into Marshall's own analysis of the situation. Having passed the test, Eisenhower was immediately promoted Brigadier General and appointed 'Action Officer' in the War Plans Division with special responsibility for operations in the Southwest Pacific. He went into action within minutes of his appointment, commandeering the British liner *Queen Mary* to transport 15,000 soldiers to Australia, organizing a convoy with naval escort to carry ammunition and more men to Brisbane to establish a supply base, and

arranging with the Treasury for $10,000,000 to be made available for the hiring of mercenaries willing to run the Japanese blockade between Australia and the Philippines, but it was too late.

On 22 December the Japanese, dominant in the air after destroying more than half the Philippines-based B-17 bombers and nearly a hundred fighters, landed forces on the northern island of Luzon. Four days later MacArthur was forced to declare Manila an open city and withdraw his forces to the Bataan Peninsula. From then on hope for the Philippines was abandoned.

Below: The explosion aboard USS *Arizona* after a bomb penetrated her forward magazine.

Eisenhower's hastily arranged relief forces never reached MacArthur through the Japanese blockade and, because American war production had scarcely begun to achieve its potential it was quite impossible to cope with lease-lend demands from the European Theater as well as with the equal demands from the American and Dutch outposts in the Pacific which were being battered by the air and naval superiority of the Japanese. Within three months hope of saving anything in the Pacific had vanished and MacArthur was ordered by President Roosevelt to escape to Australia, there to build up an American force that would eventually recapture the Philippines. That would take a long time – more than three years – and much was to happen in those years on the other side of the world. Most momentously, the conquest of the Third Reich. Toward that conquest Eisenhower had now taken his first step.

3: SURROGATE

When Eisenhower typed the words 'influence Russia to enter war' he of course knew that Russia was already in the war. Hitler's Operation Barbarossa, the invasion of the USSR, had begun at 0300 hours on 22 June 1941, and by December German forces had already smashed their way through on a 1500-mile front to the Ukraine, had taken Minsk, Smolensk and Tallinn, and laid siege to Leningrad. Eisenhower's recommendation of 'influence' was really a hope that the USSR might be persuaded to invade Manchuria and establish air bases for an all-out attack on Japan. He still hoped for that. However at the end of 1941 the Soviet Union was only just beginning to impede the German invasion. As Prime Minister Churchill said in a message to Roosevelt, 'Our Russian Allies are too heavily engaged in mortal combat to think of turning on Japanese-occupied Manchuria.'

The first meeting between Churchill and Roosevelt had taken place aboard the American cruiser *Augusta* in Placentia Bay, Newfoundland, on 9 August. The two leaders had there thrashed out the first draft of the Atlantic Charter uniting the efforts of Britain and America against Nazi aggression. 'The fact alone,' says Churchill in his history of the war, 'of the United States, still technically neutral, joining with a belligerent Power in making such a declaration, was astonishing.' In December, with America itself a belligerent nation, Churchill again met the President, this time at the White House, where they compiled an impressive document uniting the names of the 26 nations now embroiled in the fight against Germany and Japan and their satellites. This declaration of the United Nations, as Churchill remarked, could not by itself win battles; 'but it set forth who we were and what we were fighting for.' The representatives of the USSR and China were conveniently in Washington and signed immediately. The underlings of the State Department were left to collect the signatures of the other 22 nations' representatives – rather as if they were canvassing the signatories of a

get well card. Indeed the United Nations pact might aptly if irreverently be described as that very thing. If the occasion entirely lacked the formal grandeur of, for example, the signing of the Peace Treaty in the Hall of Mirrors at Versailles in June 1919, it might also lack the disastrous events to which that ceremony was a prelude.

The Washington conference had been given the code name Arcadia. Eisenhower, together with his old classmate at the Point, Mark Clark, and Walter Bedell Smith, who was to become his chief of staff, met Churchill for the first time and was noted by the Prime Minister to be 'of great cheer and ebullience.' Churchill nicknamed Mark Clark the 'American Eagle' and Bedell Smith the 'American Bulldog.' Eisenhower recorded at the time that Churchill was 'a great guy – half American on his mother's side – and one hundred percent with the President.' By that he meant that the two leaders were of one mind in their wish to achieve the main purpose of the conference: to establish the planning principle of coping with the European enemy first.

That was no easy matter. With 'the day of infamy' so close in the memory of the American nation it could scarcely be wondered at that vengeance against Japan was the most vehemently expressed emotion. The immediate practical expression of vengeance against anybody at all was severely hampered by the delayed opening to full throttle of the war machine. The army still had less than half the 4,000,000 men needed simply for defense, and of these only one division was trained and equipped. The navy had a total of only 42 capital ships, the Army Air Force only 807 planes. Roosevelt set production targets for 1942 of 60,000 planes, 45,000 tanks and 8,000,000 tons of ships, but so far as availability was concerned at the beginning of the year these figures were no more than a dream. Since, however, neither Churchill nor Roosevelt inclined

Right: Eisenhower aboard the USS *Augusta* for the Atlantic Charter meeting with Churchill and Roosevelt.

Left: Churchill and Roosevelt met again at the White House in December 1941 at the Arcadia Conference.

to the policy of sitting down and waiting for things to be made ready, they got on with establishing priorities; and the priority so far as the order of battle was concerned – as Eisenhower wholeheartedly agreed – was now 'Europe first.' The Philippines were lost and the Pacific Theater must await the buildup of an Australian-based attacking force to regain a foothold. MacArthur, not altogether unnaturally, was furious. Wilfully or self-pityingly he saw the failure of Washington to rescue the Philippines as a political maneuver in which the villainous Churchill had persuaded the indifferent Roosevelt to divert American effort to Europe.

He never forgave Eisenhower for what he saw as a stroke of personal treachery, or Marshall and the war chiefs for the 'Europe first' policy. He attracted an enormous amount of sympathy, for he was seen by the American public, who were not of course privy to the strategy behind the decisions being taken at the 12 meetings that took place between Churchill and Roosevelt during the Arcadia Conference, as a glamorous hero leading his hard-pressed troops against overwhelming odds – unhonored, unsung, and isolated from all help. A handsome man much given in his public pronouncements to rhetorical catch phrases, he was also a publicist of the first order, and never failed to reach the hearts of an applauding nation. The antithesis of Eisenhower's homespun backwoodsman, the 'rawboned gawky Kansas boy,' he was the elegant sophisticate, the daring leader with the rakishly worn General's cap and corncob pipe who shook his fist at the Japanese-occupied Philippines as the torpedo boat evacuating him and his family pulled away, bellowing mellifluously 'I shall return!' To the end of the war he persisted in the view that Washington should have dealt with Japan first.

It is now known that Japan was not anxious for a prolonged war with the Allies; it was not known then. But as the men and materials were not available for a diversion of effort it would not have made any difference anyway. The main theme of the Arcadia meetings was what *was* available and what was to be done with it.

'Most important of all,' Eisenhower wrote on one of his desk memo pads now preserved among the Eisenhower Papers: 'Firmness of the alliance. We can learn from British.'

There was certainly some experience to be drawn upon. Britain had been at war since 1939, had mobilized her military and industrial forces from what was virtually a standing start, endured the withdrawal from Dunkirk and the storming of London by the Luftwaffe, and had shown remarkable adaptability in leadership. America had only potential to offer; but as Roosevelt said in a directive to Marshall, 'It is very important to morale to give this country a feeling that they are in the war, to give Germans the reverse effect, to have American troops in active fighting across the Atlantic.' From small beginnings a mighty force could be built up 'to plunge the knife into Germany' as

Below: General Wavell's (left) overall command of India paved the way for US/British cooperation.

Churchill colorfully put it. In those words was the embryo of Operation Overlord, the invasion of the European mainland by combined American and British forces – an embryo that at the time of Arcadia was to take two-and-a-half years of painful parturition. But though they could not possibly have foreseen the eventual size of their creation, there was no doubt that even at that conceptual moment Eisenhower and Marshall had identical views on its overall direction. The British ran their war with independent strategies worked out by the Commanders in Chief of the naval, army and air forces operating in a particular battle area, concerning themselves only with local demands and conditions; but Marshall was convinced the fighting ability of a consortium such as that embraced by the United Nations pact would be greatly increased through a single commander unifying its effects. As a tryout for the principle of unification, General Sir Archibald Wavell, already commander in chief in India when the Japanese assault in the Far East had begun was appointed Supreme

Commander of ABDA (an acronym designating the American, British, Dutch, and Australian forces engaged throughout the Far East). It was an appointment intended to show Churchill that the Americans were willing – anyway in prevailing circumstances – to accept British domination. 'If the principle is established,' Eisenhower said with one of his displays of diplomatic subtlety, 'it can be applied in a different form later. If we play ball with the British now they can hardly object to playing ball with us later.'

As for Roosevelt's directive to Marshall, it was agreed that a token expedition of American troops should be sent to Northern Ireland so that the resident British force could be released for active service in some more demanding theater – most particularly the Middle East, where General Auchinleck, the Commander in Chief, had been amassing stores and forces for a big action by General Ritchie's Eighth Army against Rommel. This was planned for February. Ritchie's forces included the famous 1st Armored Division which was fully

trained and equipped for desert warfare; he also had a well-established base at Benghazi in the northwest corner of Cyrenaica, and every tactical advantage for a thrust against Rommel, who was 400 miles from his base at Tripoli. But as January passed it brought Churchill telegram after telegram from Auchinleck which revealed, often by way of dissembling phrases, that in spite of tactical advantages Ritchie was being outmaneuvered at every turn. 'It must be admitted,' Auchinleck wrote in anticipation of the withdrawal from Benghazi on 29 January, 'that the enemy has succeeded beyond his expectations and mine, and that his tactics have been skilful and bold. . . . Rommel has taken considerable risks, and so have we. So far he is justified by results, but General Ritchie and I are seeking every possible means to turn the tables on him. Losses of 1st Armored Division in tanks and men are heavy, and the fighting value of this key formation may be temporarily impaired, though I hope not.'

Unfortunately the hope was not realizable. Auchinleck laid a great deal of blame on the impotence of British tanks compared with Rommel's and reinforced it with veiled criticism of his commanders, whose tactical leadership, he said, was not 'of sufficiently high standard to offset German material advantages.' Churchill was suspicious of these explanations of a continual retreat which 'ruined our hopes and lost us Benghazi and all the stores General Auchinleck had been gathering for his hoped-for offensive.' He was never convinced that British armor that had undergone workshop overhaul at Cairo and transported across the desert on transporters to save wearing out the tracks could possibly be inferior to Rommel's; and he only grudgingly admitted that Rommel's tanks might not only be superior but that there might be more of them.

But it was not only in the Middle East that disasters were multiplying. The Japanese commanded the Pacific; Singapore fell, India was threatened. The Battle of the Atlantic raged with tremendous losses. Leningrad was besieged and starving. Three of Germany's capital ships, *Scharnhorst*, *Gneisenau*, and *Prinz Eugen* escaped through the English Channel to the safety of Norwegian waters, to the great humiliation of the British. There seemed to be no gleam of light anywhere.

As the number of disasters of early 1942 mounted they seemed to be offset only by the gradual increase of American armaments production and forces training. But against that there was renewed pressure from MacArthur's sympathizers to 'Forget the dam' British and go out and get the yellow bastards who are killing our boys and walking in on American soil.' It was no time for vacillation; and in the hope that the 'Japan now' lobby would be quietened Roosevelt and Marshall agreed to the establishment of internment camps for Japanese residents or Americans with Japanese ancestry. Eisenhower was horrified. 'How can you be working for freedom, fighting against Nazi oppres-

Below: US bombers joined the RAF in attacks on Axis supply points in North Africa from 1942.

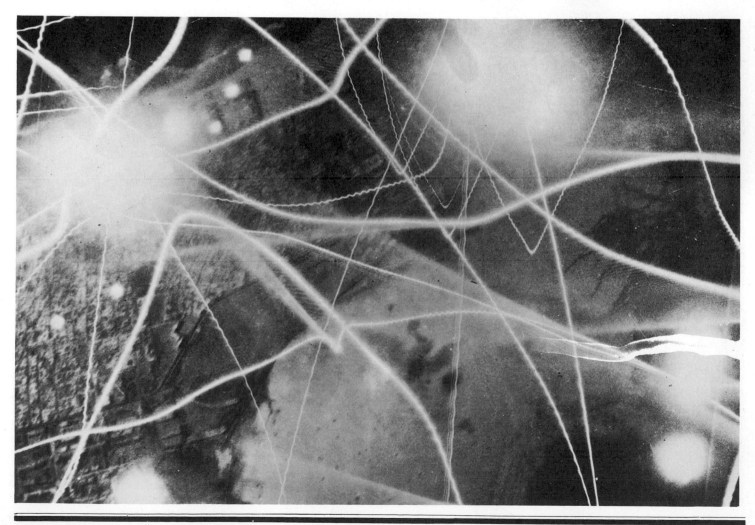

sion and suchlike, when you're keeping people locked up because they're the same skin as an enemy race. They're Americans, *citizens*.' 'Military necessity,' said Marshall drily. 'I guess even that don't justify keeping free people captive,' Eisenhower confided to Leonard Gerow, his old Fort Leavenworth classmate, who was head of the War Plans Division.

His protest went unheeded. Marshall had the same ethical objections; but, like the President, he was giving way on one issue to secure success in another – the smooth running of the Arcadia decision to defeat Hitler first. It worked. Much publicity was given in the press and on radio to the transport of alien suspects from coastal areas to inland internment camps, and there were widespread campaigns on the civilian front aimed at giving people a sense of participation in the war effort by collecting salvage of allegedly-scarce materials such as rubber, scrap iron and the like. Congressional heat was thus diverted from the firm policy of the War Plans Division. It only remained to work out more detailed plans and to put to

Churchill (now back in London) and his military advisers a scheme that would leave no doubt in British minds as to the sincerity of American commitment.

As Marshall's 'Action Officer' Eisenhower was given the task of preparing the scheme. By the end of February 1942 he had it ready. Boldly imaginative, it was the first stage in the growth of the embryo mighty force conceived 'to plunge the knife into Germany.' It was headed, with Eisenhower's typical disregard for the formal phrases of bureaucracy, 'We've got to go to Europe and fight, and we've got to quit wasting resources all over the world and – still worse – wasting time.' Equally tersely, the plan was divided into two brief sections, each headed by a question: '1. What are the vital tasks that must be performed by the United States in order to avoid defeat while offensive power is being built up; 2. Where can an eventual offensive be launched that will do most toward defeating the Axis?'

To the first question he gave an answer that was emphatic on two points: to secure the defenses of the North American continent and to continue to

Above and right: Japanese American citizens were interned on the outbreak of war. Eisenhower did not think this a justifiable action even in wartime but his protests went unheeded and some 200,000 Japanese were sent to War Relocation Authority centers.

assist Britain and the Soviet Union with Lease-Lend supplies that would enable them both to carry on the fight until America could join in. The second question was more tricky; but his answer was equally direct: through Western Europe, because such an attack would involve the shortest possible sea routes; because overland communications were superior in Western Europe to those in any other area from which the enemy could be attacked; and because England already had airfields from which a large air force could operate. 'Nowhere else,' he concluded, 'is there such a base, so favorably situated with respect to our European enemy.'

It was easy enough to get Marshall and Roosevelt to approve the plan but not so easy to convince the Commander in Chief of the United States Fleet,

Admiral Ernest King, who was something of an advocate of the 'Japan first' policy. His seaman's eye was penetrating enough to see 'attack' in the more naval form of 'invasion' and he put to Marshall and Eisenhower 'the difficulty of organizing, on the shores of Western Europe, a force of sufficient strength to meet the hostile opposition that could be brought against it.'

He had touched upon the very heart of the tactical problem of assembling the mightiest invasion fleet in history. However, the more immediate problem was that Eisenhower's plan, bold though it was, lacked the forces to implement it. It had to be sold to the British with the proviso that no important contribution of American help, other than Lease-Lend, could be given during 1942. In the event it was not Eisenhower who had to

do the selling. Marshall himself, together with Roosevelt's personal envoy, Harry Hopkins, went to London, leaving Eisenhower in charge of the War Plans Division. His command had been authorized by the President and on 28 March 1942 he was promoted to the rank of Major General and told by Marshall, 'You are now my subordinate commander.'

Right: Admiral King (left) advocated a Japan-first policy, rather than Eisenhower's Europe-first principle.

Far right: In 1942 Eisenhower was promoted to Major General.

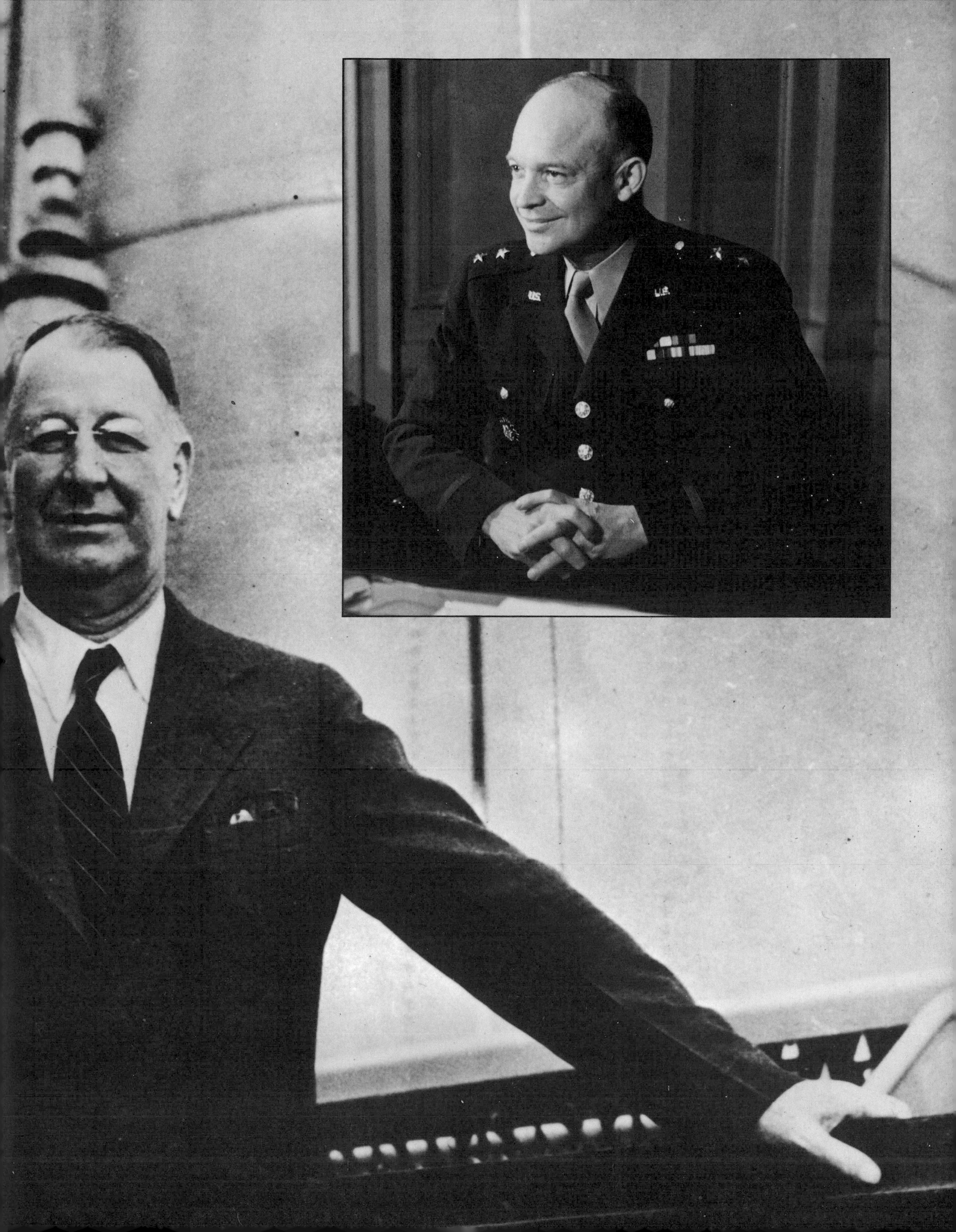

Left: Eisenhower enjoys a hasty roadside meal of 'C' rations which has been kept hot on the engine.

4:TURNING POINT

The year 1942 saw ceaseless activity for Eisenhower as for everyone else concerned in planning and fighting the war. In retrospect it can be seen as the turning point at which the fortunes of the Allies began to rise and those of the Axis to fall; but those enduring its vicissitudes were too busy with immediate problems to be aware of a sense of history. The only significant indication of awareness was the official change of title from War Plans Division to Operations Division. 'We were no longer planning; we were in business,' Roosevelt wrote.

At the beginning of the year Eisenhower wrote to a colleague, Major General LeRoy Lutes, who was about to join the staff of the War Plans Division (as it still was at that time), 'Just to give you an inkling of the kind of madhouse you are getting into, it is now eight o'clock New Year's Eve. I have a couple hours' work ahead of me, and tomorrow will be no different from today. I have been here about three weeks and this noon I had my first luncheon outside of the office.' His usual fare, eaten at his desk, was a raw-beef sandwich with onions and pepper, a hamburger or a hot dog. His only links with his family were occasional phone conversations with Mamie, often interrupted by incoming teletypes, dashed-off notes to his mother in Abilene and brief contact with his brother Milton and his wife; for when Eisenhower was not forced by the demands of service to spend his nights on a camp bed in his office he would drive across the Potomac to Church Falls, Virginia, where Milton lived and worked in the Department of Agriculture. Even the family sorrow of their father's death on 10 March could not be regarded as a first call on Eisenhower's attention. He wrote despairingly, 'I should so much like to be with my Mother these few days. But we're at war! And war is not soft – it has no time to indulge even the deepest and most sacred emotions.' He granted himself half an hour with his phones off the

hook and his office door locked, 'to have that much time, by myself, to think of him . . . he was a just man, well liked, well educated, a thinker. He was undemonstrative, quiet, modest and of exemplary habits . . . an uncomplaining person in the face of adversity, and such plaudits as were accorded to him did not inflate his ego . . . it was always so difficult to let him know the depth of my affection for him.' The touching little encomium was rounded off with the words 'I love my Dad.'

The optimism of Roosevelt's cheery note about being in business proved to be slightly ahead of justification. Throughout the year in which events were, so to speak, surreptitiously working for the ultimate triumph of Overlord, there was a great deal of indication to the contrary. The statesmen and military leaders of the principal Allies met again and again in London, Washington and elsewhere. They hammered away at plans that were forever changing and being changed – sometimes as a consequence of the exigencies of a particular theater of war, sometimes by way of clashes of personality. The most frequent changes were forced by continual pressure of the Russians to mount an all-out attack on Germany. As the months went by and envoy succeeded envoy, conference succeeded conference and arguments, cogent and otherwise, for attack and delay were filed in the records, that pressure came to inspire the three urgent words – Second Front Now!

The urgency was in a way understandable. The German invasion had been followed by the siege of Leningrad (to last an eventual 900 days), and in the six months between June and December 1941 there were 3,500,000 Russian casualties. No sign of any reversal of disaster was seen until after the battle of Stalingrad and the surrender of the German Sixth Army in December 1942. In December 1941 the Soviet Union formed a vast battleground with only Premier Stalin's scorched-earth policy halting the German advance on Moscow. His furious outbursts against the United States and Britain for their slowness in forcing the Germans to withdraw their armies from the Soviet Union to deal with an attack in the west went on and on. They were to some extent the result of consciousness of his own faults as Commander in Chief of the armed forces of the USSR. His prewar neglect of armaments production had forced him to buy time from Hitler in 1939 by signing the pact dealing with the partition of Poland – a pact that, predictably, resulted in betrayal; and his unwise distribution of his defending divisions along the western borders of the Soviet Union had left them extremely vulnerable. It was easy to hide his faults behind a continual stream of accusations of Allied sloth and ignore the events of history. He argued that if Britain and France had stemmed the German blitzkrieg Hitler would have been too occupied on the western front to attack Russia. It was a circular argument of ifs and buts which offered no resolution. But the argument, the ranting and railing, and the insistent demand for immediate action to aid Russia was, Eisenhower said, 'Like a jungle drum.'

One of the drummers was Vyacheslav Molotov, Stalin's envoy to a conference 'for an exchange of views on the organization of a second front in Europe in the near future.' That was in May 1942. He was given a sumptuous room on the

Below: Roosevelt met Molotov in 1942 and agreed to open a second front.

family floor of the White House, investigated every corner of it for bugging devices, and slept in it with a pistol under his pillow – not what one would call a friendly guest.

'At the conference,' Eisenhower recalled, 'Mr Molotov managed to extract from the President some sort of promise about a second front in 1942, even though George Marshall and Ernest King both went all out on emphasizing the problems – shortage of shipping, production, need for heavy planning etc. Also our supplies to England had to be kept up.'

Whatever the Chiefs' warnings, the pledge was given and turned into an official communiqué: 'In the course of the conversations full understanding was reached with regard to the urgent tasks of creating a Second Front in 1942.' Thus two of the urgent and harrying words were turned into a catchphrase that screened the woolliness of the pledge itself. In London, Churchill instantly identified the inherent dangers of the communiqué, dissociated himself from it, and gruffly told Molotov that there was no way in which a cross-channel invasion could be launched in 1942. Nevertheless, on his arrival back in Moscow Molotov waved the documentary evidence of the success of his mission as jubilantly as Chamberlain had waved his 'peace in our time' message in 1938. In doing so he gave Stalin

and the Supreme Soviet a weapon which was to be turned again and again against the United States and Britain in retribution for their alleged defection. For the moment the scene of action was shifted elsewhere.

The shift was on 21 June 1942, the very day that Eisenhower and Mark Clark, his designated deputy, had an afternoon talk with Churchill, who was again at the White House, about the cross-channel invasion part of the Second Front. 'Mr C.,' Eisenhower recorded, 'was quite unequivocal about the earliest possible date being 1943.'

Churchill's bluntness, emphasized with stabbing motions of his cigar, is not surprising. Before lunch he had been talking with Roosevelt when a startling telegram had arrived: 'Tobruk has surrendered with 25,000 men taken prisoner.' Seeing Churchill wince, the President said expansively, 'What can we do to help?' as if Churchill had only to flick the ashes of his cigar off and ask for the entire output of the United States arsenal. 'Give us as many Sherman tanks as you can spare and ship them to the Middle East as quickly as possible,' he replied. 'Something easier said than done,' Marshall pointed out – only too truly, for there had been many delays in design and production, partly owing to the tardiness of the tank's acceptance in the interwar years. Nevertheless Churchill should have them. 'He growled his thanks in the words *noblesse oblige*,' Eisenhower recorded on his desk pad.

Apart from the help promised to Auchinleck in the Middle East the day was in another sense a noteworthy one. Churchill placed his bets on Eisenhower and Clark being leading figures in the forthcoming invasion and gave each of them a copy of his memorandum on the subject, which he had prepared before coming to Washington. The operation had been codenamed Roundup and Eisenhower was to record later that between it and Overlord there were only 'the differences generated by time and place.'

The memorandum was an example of Churchill's remarkable grasp of military strategy. It emphasized that the three qualities of 'magnitude, simultaneity, and violence' would above all be needed. There would have to be mystification of the enemy by a number of feint attacks

Right: The bitter fighting in the east and massive Russian losses hastened the plans for the invasion of Europe.

so that the Luftwaffe would be dispersed and uncertain where its chief effort should be concentrated. The main Allied attack would be in the Pas de Calais area, the misleading ones in Belgium, Holland, Denmark and on the Cotentin peninsula. He thought the first wave of Allied invaders should include at least 10 armored brigades, which would obviously be subjected to very high risks and great losses but would also create 'great disorder' into which the second wave would be launched at smaller cost. Assuming that the enemy would need at least a week to recover their balance, the Allied air force must establish bases on enemy airfields as soon as they were captured. The capture of at least four ports was also vital to ensure that the assault troops had uninterrupted supplies. Not only the assault forces had to be considered: there would need to be a third wave of at least 300,000 infantry with their own artillery so that the assault forces could be consolidated and formed into proper corps and divisions. Once that was achieved the campaign 'would follow the normal and conventional lines of organization and supply' and the commander would be able to direct operations from a position of strength.

Churchill had good reason for thinking that Eisenhower would be one of the leading figures in the invasion, for on 21 June Eisenhower was in the middle of preparing to hand over his job as Marshall's surrogate and depart for Europe as a field commander. Marshall had sent him to London at the end of May to discuss with the British Chiefs of Staff the build up and organization of the American forces who were to be sent to Europe in consequence of Roosevelt's insistence that American troops should be involved 'in active fighting across the Atlantic' and Eisenhower's own declaration that 'We've got to go to Europe and fight' – in short the prelude to Roundup/Overlord. The impression he had made on the Chiefs was, with a single exception, so favorable that upon his return to Washington he was appointed by Roosevelt on Marshall's recommendation 'Commander of United States Forces

European Theater of Operations' and told to prepare to leave in a few days.

It was news that he could scarcely credit. Only six months earlier, by Marshall's word he had been 'completely condemned to a desk job in Washington for the duration.' But Marshall's word was not as unchanging as his icy austerity. 'It does not do for a soldier to be inflexible,' he said on the eve of Eisenhower's departure to take up his appointment in London. 'Anyway, Bolero [codename for the American forces buildup program] was your baby. Feed it and educate it.'

Once over the shock of the appointment Eisenhower mused on its importance, confiding his thoughts as usual to a pad of yellow copy paper: 'It's a big job – if U.S.-U.K. stay squarely behind Bolero and go after it tooth and nail, it will be the biggest American job of the war. Of course command now does not necessarily mean command in the operation – but the job before the battle begins will be the biggest outside that of the Supremo himself.' He wrote to his mother that night telling her that the papers for his promotion to the rank of lieutenant general were on the President's desk.

The so-called 'first' American soldier to land in Britain was Milburn Henke, a cheerfully grinning private from Minnesota who was pictured in all the popular newspapers on 26 January 1942 disembarking from a transport ship at Belfast and being greeted by the King's

personal representative and chiefs from all the services. He was in fact far from being the first, but from the publicity angle it was of no consequence. Long before the public relations popularity of the word 'image' both British and American governments were trying to create one for the GI. Newspapers, the radio and official handouts were given the job of establishing a rapport between soldiers of the two armies and between the GIs and the civilian population. It was no easy task. Embattled and tightly rationed Britain did not at first take kindly to the seemingly aggressive GI with his high pay (five times that of the British soldier), abundant food and luxuries that had long disappeared. Conversely the Americans found British reserve difficult to overcome and the national laconic humor offensive. The famous anonymous comment on the GI that he was 'over-paid, over-fed, over-sexed and over here' did not seem like the welcome to be given to the relief force who had come to rescue the British from an overpowering enemy, but the Britishers' view of their rescuers was colored by reminiscences of 1917 and the doughboys' late arrival, as well as of America's more recent isolationism which only Pearl Harbor had changed. Abrasiveness succored by ignorance needed more effective treatment than could be given by official public relations exercises. Eisenhower provided that treatment.

When he arrived in London on 24 June 1942 he declared publicly that he was 'a simple Kansas small-town boy.' A Guards officer on the liaison staff was reported to have added 'And he's brought all the corn of Kansas with him.' There was truth behind the malice. Eisenhower dealt in clichés, perhaps without realizing that they were part of the lingua franca of emotion, just as were Churchill's carefully coined rhetorical phrases. He had an abundant flow of them. At his headquarters in Grosvenor Square his talks to the headquarter's staff officers assigned to him were rich with such phrases as 'determined enthusiasm and optimism,' 'work hard, assume responsibility, and be cheerful,' 'team spirit,' 'we need imagination and initiative and a lot of it,' 'we must all pull together' and 'I want a big crowd of friends around here because no successful staff can have personal enemies.' They were hackneyed phrases but Eisenhower's wide grin and amiability could invest such clichés with charm and conviction. Within days he had virtually everyone on his side. Those who remained antagonistic were those who in the end had to be returned across the Atlantic, for Eisen-

Below: Eisenhower led Operation Torch but thought it would divert resources and delay the invasion of Europe.

hower had no ability for delving into people's psyches and unravelling the talents behind them. If they did not suit him he sent them back and asked Marshall for replacements. He could not of course do that with the enlisted men who since January had been pouring into the country, or with his opposite numbers in the British forces, but with the GIs there was little difficulty. Apart from the stars on his shoulders he was one of them – he knew it and they knew it. It was to be famously reported in 1945, on the eve of the Rhine crossing, that a young GI by chance encountered Eisenhower and was asked 'How are you feeling, son?' The boy recognized the commander and answered honestly, 'Awful nervous, General. I don't feel good at all.' To which Eisenhower equally honestly replied, 'I'm nervous too. Maybe if we walk along together to the river we'll be good for each other.' It was only one of numerous examples of the fellow feeling that attracted others to him.

However, not all were attracted. There were those who repeated Patton's accusation of bonhomie being a cover up for an inferiority complex. More unfortunate at British command level was the critical attitude of Chief of the Imperial

General Staff General Sir Alan Brooke, who thought Eisenhower was an amiable buffoon with no sense of strategy and little practical ability. It was not a good basis for a relationship between the two top men of the English-speaking armies, and Eisenhower knew it. However, being a man who tended to say nothing unless he could say something agreeable, he said nothing. The clash of personalities – for however courteously disguised by protocol it might be, there was undoubtedly a clash – was to lead to tension and dissension in the echelons of command. The public naturally remained in ignorance of such difficulties. They took to their hearts the general who visited every GI camp and air base and poured out his jolly phrases about team spirit and working together and the need for imagination when fraternizing with 'these Britishers who've had a helluva rougher time than you've had to date.' He encouraged them to save some of their pay and invest it in war bonds instead of 'flashing it around like you're all Pierpont Morgans,' and he directed commanding officers to toughen up their men physically and in the matter of discipline. 'At the end of a whistle-stop of eight bases I counted I'd had three salutes – and those were

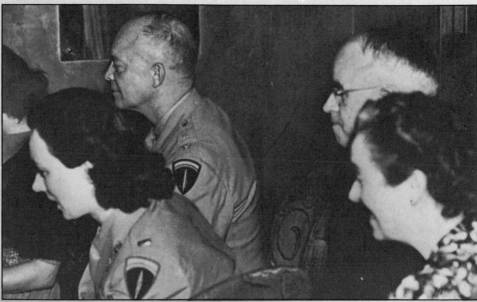

from Britishers. I'm directing this theater and I'm hiving off those commanding officers who can't run a disciplined base. Their dossiers aren't going to look so good.' There was, as Churchill was to note, an iron hand in the velvet glove.

Eisenhower was assisted in his difficult task by two men. Harry Butcher, a peacetime PRO risen to vice-president of the Columbia Broadcasting System and just before Eisenhower's departure from Washington seconded from the

Navy Reserve, was his personal assistant under the uniformed guise of 'naval aide.' He was no *eminence grise*; rather, he was something of a gentleman's gentleman. He was always around to write up Eisenhower's diary, play gin rummy with him, give him gags for his speeches, advise him on the more difficult aspects of public relations and in general act as off-duty companion and helpmate in times of trouble. The other, more pacifying hand was that of Kay

Above left and above: Kay Summersby was Eisenhower's chauffeuse. Her alleged affair with Eisenhower caused a major scandal when she published her autobiography after the war.

Summersby, ex-model, ex-movie extra and ex-wife, enlisted in the transport section of the Women's Army Corps and allotted to Eisenhower as his driver because of her encyclopedic knowledge of London. 'She is also very pretty,'

Right: US troops entering Oran on 10 November 1942 during the landings in French North Africa.

Right: US troops entering Oran on 10 November 1942 during the landings in French North Africa.

Eisenhower told Mamie artlessly in a letter. 'Irish and slender and I think in process of getting a divorce. But she's efficient, which is all that worries me.' Harry Butcher discreetly forgot to mail the letter. He recorded in the diary that 'Ike defines this member of the W.A.C. as "a double-breasted G.I. with a built-in foxhole" ' – which sounds more like the invention of PRO Butcher than of the country lad from Kansas. All the same, the affair lasted romantically until 1945. In 1948 Kay Summersby published a book called *Eisenhower Was My Boss* but threatened to reveal what she called 'my real story' in a series of articles in *Look* magazine. The affair caused a lot of sniggering gossip when Eisenhower ran for President.

Below: The 1st US Ranger Battalion on the march near Arzev, on 12 December 1942.

Others who administered to his well-being were his Irish batman, Master Sergeant Micky McKeogh, who had been a bellhop at the New York Plaza; his WAC secretary Captain Mattie Pinnett; his tailor Sergeant Mike Popp and a dozen cooks and office auxiliaries. Most important of all was Major-General Walter Bedell Smith, now Eisenhower's Chief of Staff, a high-powered personality, and an extremely capable administrator who could play Machievelli one minute and Malvolio the next, according to the advantages to be gained for the cause in general and Eisenhower in particular. Butcher was the organizer of creature comforts, Smith of military and diplomatic maneuvers. These, once Eisenhower was installed at 20 Grosvenor Square and in the cottage at Richmond Park in Surrey where he relaxed at weekends, moved through a

maze of political intrigue and military ramifications toward Eisenhower's first experience on the field of battle. He noted with some amusement that he was '52 years old, 27 of them as a professional soldier, and heading for action at last!'

Complex though the ramifications and machinations of the politicians and generals were, they took only a few weeks to come to a head. Auchinleck's dispatches from the Western Desert continued as harbingers of disaster, with retreat to El Alamein following the fall of Tobruk. Churchill, under heavy fire in Parliament for his handling of affairs in general and those of the Middle East in particular, found a scapegoat in Auchinleck, whom he replaced with

Generals Alexander and Montgomery. In Moscow he again spoke out against Roosevelt's foolishly-given promise for a Second Front in 1942 and roused Stalin's interest in a diversionary action – the invasion of French North Africa by American and British forces, an idea of Roosevelt's to fulfil his pledge that American troops would be 'involved in active fighting across the Atlantic' during 1942. It was an idea that to Churchill was highly suspect because it involved collaboration with the Vichy government of Marshal Pétain, whose defeatist attitude had brought about the surrender of France in 1940. Churchill was much closer in character and purpose to Charles de Gaulle, exiled to England as leader of the Free French and calling himself head of the true French government. But events in the Middle East forced Churchill's hand despite sounds of alarm voiced by his military advisers, who told him that the buildup of forces necessary for a North African campaign would inevitably delay the main invasion of Europe. Undaunted, he switched to

Roosevelt's way of thinking and argued that if a diversionary attack was made in North Africa, then German armies would have to be withdrawn from Russia to back Rommel in his fight for the essential port of Alexandria. This bit of political doublethink naturally pleased Stalin, who more or less willingly conceded that the true second front would in the end benefit from the delay. Subsequent events turned him against the scheme, but Churchill's unexpectedly friendly meeting with him seemed a godsend at the time.

That was on 13 August, a week after Eisenhower had been appointed Commander in Chief of the Allied Expeditionary Force that was to invade French North Africa (Operation Torch) and had noted delightedly that he was 'heading for action at last.' His delight stemmed from a natural but as it turned out somewhat naïve assumption that as commander in chief his plans for Torch would be acknowledged as the design of a professional soldier appointed to make them and acted upon accordingly. 'I

Above: Captured German transport lined up outside Tobruk while gasoline-storage tanks burn in the town.

couldn't have been further from the truth,' he recorded later. 'The politicians are wrangling.' Indeed they were, but so were the heads of the armies, navies, and air forces.

The main strategical argument was about where the invasion forces should strike, the British Chiefs of Staff pressing for landings on the Mediterranean coast, the Americans insisting on the Atlantic coast. The matter was resolved eventually by Roosevelt and Churchill, who had agreed that there should be an Atlantic coast landing at Casablanca and three other landings at the Algerian port of Oran, Algiers and, after Algiers was in Allied hands, Bône. Once Bône had fallen there would be a good striking-off point for the drive eastward into Tunisia and Libya to meet and destroy the Axis forces being driven westward by a new offensive by Montgomery's Eighth Army. This pincer movement, it was claimed, would destroy all the Axis

forces in North Africa, relieve Malta and ensure the safety of the Mediterranean for Allied shipping. General Marshall was not sanguine about a quick conquest. 'The enemy knows what holding on to North Africa means to him. He'll fight tooth and claw. I can't see us making it before spring. And that'll mean no chance of a cross-Channel invasion in 1943.' Thus the real Second Front was in effect postponed by the decision for Torch – 'Which is just what I told you,' Marshall pointed out with some ire to those of the opposite persuasion.

It was also what the enemy assumed. Axis Intelligence had been definite in its conclusion that a strike by the Allies against either French North Africa or Europe was extremely unlikely before the spring of 1943. If such an attack came earlier, it was thought, it would be most likely to fall in Libya in an effort to reinforce the Eighth Army's efforts

Right: The first French prisoners are brought in by American troops in North Africa.

to push the Afrika Korps out from the rear, or on the fine harbor at Dakar in French West Afrika, which offered a worthwhile prize. So it was there that Hitler ordered defensive measures to be taken. The Allies were well aware of this. Therefore it was doubly important that Axis suspicions regarding an attack on Dakar should be encouraged and British Counter-Intelligence arranged many misleading ploys to encourage them. That the secret of Torch was well kept is obvious from *Inside Hitler's Headquarters*, in which Hitler's Deputy Chief of Staff, General Walter Warlimont, says, 'No adequate information could be provided either by our own Intelligence service or that of the Italian High Command. . . . Neither we nor the Italians had any conception that the landing was . . . imminent.'

The strategy of the landings was but a tiny part of the overall problem which Eisenhower had to face. The situation *vis-à-vis* the French – both Free and Vichy – was farcically complex. An American diplomatic relationship with the Vichy government had been maintained through an Ambassador, Admiral William Leahy, and an envoy in Algiers, Robert Murphy, and Roosevelt con-

Above: General de Gaulle arrives in North Africa. He did not receive US support until after the landings.

sidered it unwise to enlist the help of Charles de Gaulle's anti-Vichy Free French. There was in any case no love lost between him and de Gaulle. He refused even to allow Churchill to tell him that the invasion of French North Africa was being mounted. Churchill was naturally uncomfortable about 'the gravity of the affront which [de Gaulle] would have to suffer by being deliberately excluded from all share in the design. . . . As some means of softening this slight to him, I arranged to confide the trustee-ship of Madagascar into his hands as a consolation prize.'

If de Gaulle was not to be the figurehead round whom the vacillating Moroccan and Algerian populations might be rallied to aid Allied landings, who else was there? Robert Murphy, who was as knowledgeable as anyone regarding the intrigues centered in Algiers, endorsed the suggestion that General Henri Giraud, an anti-Vichy Frenchman who had been captured by the Germans in 1940 but had audaciously escaped from prison and was now living near Lyons, was the ideal choice. Giraud was already in close secret liaison with the Chief of Staff of the French forces in Algiers, General Charles Mast and, Murphy said, needed only transport to bring him to Algiers to confer with Eisenhower's military staff. That simple and necessary requirement was in fact very far from being the only thing Giraud wanted. He proposed to demand nothing less than to usurp Eisenhower's command of the Allied forces and to insist on an invasion not only of North Africa but of unoccupied France also. In short, he was under a complete misapprehension about Allied capabilities and intentions and conceitedly supposed that

his name had far more value in terms of glamorous leadership than General Mark Clark was convinced of. Clark, who was Eisenhower's deputy, was reported as saying, 'I'd say Giraud's pulling power is virtually nil.' He was right. Giraud was a far from magical figure as a catalyst. Nonetheless he was sent for and an extraordinarily complex maneuver undertaken to get him by plane to Gibraltar and thence by a British submarine commanded by an American naval officer to a coastal villa between Algiers and Oran. There General Clark and his staff had inexplicably fixed the rendezvous, though Eisenhower himself was at his headquarters in Gibraltar and there was no apparent need for cloak-and-dagger maneuvers. The ludicrous nature of those maneuvers was

emphasized by a surprise visit by the Algerian police during the conference, necessitating a speedy descent by Clark and his colleagues into the cellar while Murphy convinced the gendarmerie that there was nothing more interesting going on than a party given by the Americans for some local cabaret ladies. Even more farcically, General Clark lost his trousers in the battering his small boat suffered during its return to the submarine through heavy seas. Looking back, Eisenhower was to write of the events being 'like a Mack Sennett comedy film,' but at the time he was far from amused.

While the conference was going on the invasion fleet was approaching. There were still many more connivances to be made with the French in an effort to bring them to the Allied side. Per-

sonalities involved in the plot and counterplot included the Vichy collaborators Pétain, Laval and Admiral Darlan, who was Commander in Chief of all Vichy forces and Pétain's deputy; and the anti-Vichy commander in chief, General Juin, and his colleagues General Béthouart and Admiral Michelier. Their involvement was spread over a period of days – in some cases weeks – before the date set for the landings, Sunday 8 November. The Allies had hoped to persuade Darlan to divert his loyalty away from Vichy so that the main body of the French fleet, which had been impotently anchored at the Toulon naval base since the armistice of 1940, could be brought in on the Allied side. Darlan's treacherous nature was well known, but Churchill had been quite

willing to make obeisances to him – or, anyway, to have the Americans do so: 'Kiss Darlan's ass if you have to, but get the French navy,' was the phrase he used to Eisenhower. The duplicity of the idea behind the phrase was quite foreign to Eisenhower's unsubtle nature, though the more Machiavellian Bedell Smith convinced him of its wisdom, but it was a phrase well in keeping with the mood of a statesman puffed with success. Churchill had every reason to feel elated. His appointment of Montgomery to lead the Eighth Army against the Afrika Corps had proved justified. The battle of El Alamein had resulted in a dispatch:

After 12 days of heavy and violent fighting the Eighth Army has in-

flicted a severe defeat on the German and Italian forces under Rommel's command. The enemy's front has broken, and British armored formations in strength have passed through and are operating in the enemy's rear areas. Such portions of the enemy's forces as can get away are in full retreat, and are being harassed by our armored and mobile forces and by our air forces. Other enemy forces are still in position, endeavoring to stave off defeat, and these are likely to be surrounded and cut off. The RAF have throughout given superb support to land battle, and are bombing the

Below: Allied Sherman tanks move up during the advance on Kasserine, Tunisia, in February 1943.

enemy's retreating columns incessantly. Fighting continues.

To this Churchill replied in typically rhetorical terms of congratulation on 6 November, adding that the victory was of 'great value to our friends in the Torch area.' 'It may be, but Ike doesn't see it that way,' Harry Butcher recorded in the diary. 'He has other things on his mind.'

The Torch invasion fleet comprised in all some 500 transports and supply ships escorted by 350 warships. These were divided into three task forces. The Western Task Force was entirely American and was commanded by Major General George Patton. In it were two infantry divisions and an armored division which had been transported from Norfolk, Virginia, in October and had crossed the Atlantic 'without let or hindrance' as the official record had it. The Western Task Force was designated to land at Safi, Fedala, and Port Lyautey on the Moroccan coast, close on and capture Casablanca and then drive westward across Morocco to link with the Center Task Force, which was concerned with capturing the Algerian port of Oran.

Center Task Force also was wholly American – mainly the 1st Infantry and 1st Armored Divisions – and had been training in Ireland and Scotland as II Corps since August. They sailed from the Clyde in ships of the Royal Navy commanded by Commodore Sir Thomas Troubridge on 22 October. The commander of the task force was Major General Lloyd Fredendall, who modelled himself on Patton but managed to create only the superficial appearance and bombastic manner of the 'blood and guts' General. In performance he was much more cautious. He was also a pronounced Anglophobe with a particular dislike for the British General in command of the Eastern Task Force, Lieutenant General Kenneth Anderson. His violent antipathies were by no means confined to the British. He was continually in open disagreement with one of his own divisional commanders, Major General Orlando Ward (of 1st Armored Division), who equally loathed the sight of him, and he demonstrated nothing but contempt for the defending population, whom he referred to as 'a pack of wog bastards with military ideas belonging to the year of the dodo.'

Anderson's force was more than half British and it had been transported from Britain entirely in ships of the Royal Navy commanded by Rear Admiral Sir Harold Burrough. As from the very first it had been assumed the Vichy forces would be less hostile to American troops, the plan was for the bulk of the British element (now to be called the British First Army) to remain in Gibraltar while their objective of Algiers was taken by an American infantry division (the 34th) in a commando assault led by the American Major General Charles Ryder. This rather transparent subterfuge was supposed to mislead the French defenders into assuming that the invaders were all American. It could scarcely have done so, for at least a third of the assault was in fact British – and, at that, included the commando troops who would be the first to land.

Admiral Sir Andrew Cunningham had been appointed naval commander in chief under Eisenhower and had entire charge of the safety and direction of the huge armada throughout the operation. His Mediterranean Fleet could scare away the Italian navy and deal with any U-Boat attacks; but no enemy shipping at any stage attempted to attack the invasion task forces, all of which arrived at their appointed rendezvous on time – a fact Patton exasperatingly refused to acknowledge, telling the naval commanders at the pre-D-Day conference on 7 November, 'Never in history has the navy landed the army at the right time and place.' This was so patently inaccurate that Cunningham merely raised an eyebrow.

Other eyebrows were raised at the same conference, for General Giraud had been inflexible in his determination to take over complete command in exchange for the value of his name as a rallying point for the French – and, of course, for his senior rank. No one except Robert Murphy was convinced of the bartering power of the name Giraud and the command was in any case not within Eisenhower's power to change, even if he had wanted to, which of course he did not. After arguing all through the night, however, Giraud ungraciously conceded the point and accepted a promise of the leadership of the French forces and governorship of North Africa – after the success of the operation.

By that time the first landings had already been made – not by any means smoothly, and certainly not at the scheduled time, which was 0100 hours for the Center Task Force. The assault troops of that force had evidently re-

Below: Eisenhower at HQ with Harry Butcher, his naval aide and old friend, and ER Lee.

ceived insufficient training. They disembarked from their transports at points east and west of Oran as if they were going on a day trip to some seaside resort. The ships' tannoys were broadcasting a commentary on a New York football game and a great deal more attention was being given to this than to the instructions being given to the guides who were supposed to go ashore first. The assault craft were mainly Higgins Boats constructed of plywood which had no more resistance to offshore rocks than paper – as was quickly discovered when some of them foundered. The LCMs (Landing Craft Mechanized) bearing the tanks of 1st Armored Division were almost equally vulnerable and many of them got stuck on sandbars near the shore. As for the aircraft that were supposed to land paratroops to capture airfields south and west of Oran, many of them were poorly navigated or set adrift by capricious winds over Spain, for they seem to have dropped their paratroopers as inconveniently distant from their objectives as possible.

The confusion regarding the response of the French – succinctly put by Patton as 'Will the sods fight or won't they?' – was still manifest. The confusion was added to rather than lessened by the unexpected presence of Admiral Darlan in Algiers – quite fortuitously and with no more to do with the war than his summarily requested presence at the bedside of his sick son, who was suspected of having poliomyelitis. Thus, while a bewildering number of politically expedient 'arrangements' was tried, none had actually been completed. Nor had the alert been given to any of the coastal-defense troops, or even to their gunners – though one or two of these had opened fire at random in the Oran area. In more warlike circumstances the assault troops would surely have suffered considerable losses if not complete failure, but as things were, fortune favored the slipshod, and the first landings were accomplished successfully, if raggedly, before the defenders were aware of them. It was then about 0300 hours and the small direct assault that had been planned to seize the port of Oran itself and the French ships in it went ahead. The assault party comprised 500 American troops aboard two coastguard cutters commanded by British naval officers. They made their approach

Above: Laval, seen here on trial in 1945, opposed Darlan's reconciliation with the Allies.

successfully. Lights ashore were still burning, since the country was still technically at peace. That state was not to last long. Suddenly the harbor lights went out and air-raid warnings sounded. A coastguard searchlight was switched on and the two cutters were caught in its glare, as were the American flags flying from the bows; but the value of these as deterrents to the defenders seemed to have been grossly overestimated. Shellfire from the coastal batteries and machine guns began at once, and a French destroyer emerged from the corner of the harbor and opened fire. Despite this merciless opposition one of the two cutters, *Walney*, got into harbor while the other, *Hartland*, drew the fire. It was hopeless, however, and both vessels were destroyed. Of the 694 soldiers and sailors in this suicidal mission only 47 escaped death or injury, and those fell prisoner. The leader of the attack, Captain FT Peters, RN, was posthumously awarded the Victoria Cross.

Meanwhile, the diplomatic crosstalk had been coming to a head in various headquarters. In Algiers Robert Murphy had hoped to persuade General Juin, who commanded the French military forces, to abandon any resistance to the American landings and Juin had indeed undertaken to aid the invasion in this way. The chance presence of Darlan made it impossible for him to do so. Darlan was Commander in Chief of all Vichy forces and Pétain's deputy. His authority was supreme. Even though

he had been toying with the idea of selling out Vichy France to his own advantage this was not the moment to do so. The attacks had come too surprisingly. 'Whatever thoughts he might have nourished of aiding an Anglo-American occupation of North-West Africa,' Churchill wrote, 'he was still bound to Pétain in form and fact. He knew that if he went over to the Allies he would become personally responsible for the inevitable invasion and occupation by Germany of unoccupied France. The most he could be prevailed upon to do, therefore, was to ask Pétain by telegram for liberty of action. In the hideous plight in which he had become involved by the remorseless chain of events this was his only course.' Although he sent a telegram, indeed a flow of telegrams, their purpose was overtaken by events. The landings by the Eastern Task Force east and west of Algiers had gone ahead more or less according to plan, though as at Oran there had been a certain amount of confusion. The direct attack on the harbor, though – again with the object of seizing the anchored French vessels and a power station ashore – was relatively successful. By 0730 hours Darlan was telegraphing Pétain to tell him that 'Landings have been carried out by American troops and British ships at Algiers and in the neighborhood.

The defenses have repulsed the attacks in several places, in particular in the port and at the naval headquarters. In other places landings have been effected by surprise and with success. The situation is getting worse and the defenses will soon be overwhelmed. Reports indicate that massive unloadings are in preparation.'

As for the Western Task Force, their landings had taken place according to plan at 0500 hours. General Patton's lack of faith in the navy's ability had again been completely unjustified. But he substituted plenty of criticism of his own forces, which he vented with characteristic spleen, though it was hardly the combat troops' fault that both they and their landing craft had been overloaded or that their supplies and armor were piling up on the beaches instead of going forward. Once again, however, lack of direction and diplomatic confusion on the defenders' side aided the invaders. There was a little resistance at Safi on the right wing of the Moroccan coast attack, but the garrison was held only by a handful of French troops who were quickly overpowered and whose far from negligible efforts were hampered by panic-stricken Arab civilians.

The invaders' advance toward Casablanca, some 140 miles up the coast, then continued throughout the day and was delayed only by the slowness of the supplies and tank support in catching up with the unopposed troops.

Meanwhile, on the left wing at Port Lyautey, 50 miles north of Casablanca, a motley crew of 3000 Moroccans, Foreign Legionnaires and Berbers put up a spirited fight from the Kasbah, a heavily defended fort at the marshy mouth of the River Sabou, which was itself a formidable obstacle to the airfield that was the assault-party's objective. But the resistance was overcome – in the main by the skilled handling of a destroyer, *Dallas*, in the shallow marshes of the Sabou from which vantage point its guns quickly vanquished those of the fort so that there was little delay in capturing the airfield. At Fedala, 15 miles north of Casablanca itself and the point of concentration of Patton's main attack, there was a conveniently anchored French battleship, *Jean Bart*, which was immobile but had a bristling display of 15-inch guns. It was of course a considerable threat to the approaching armada but was put temporarily out of action when an American shell hit a

vital part of the guns' coordinating mechanism. Both French and American aircraft then came into action – the French making strafing attacks to hold the attention of the American escort cruisers while seven French destroyers and eight submarines were hurriedly sent from Casablanca itself to attack the escort ships and transports. That attempt failed in a brief but violent sea battle in which five of the French ships and 1000 of their men were lost, compared with three killed and 25 wounded on the American side.

It is impossible, in considering Torch, to avoid the reminiscent shadow of the Gallipoli landings of 1915. Unlike that historic disaster it was successful – anyway in its first stage; but the political conspiracies and resulting delays in getting the French into action had brought about the success rather than had the planning and execution. It was all very well for Churchill to observe that a great invasion required the qualities of magnitude, simultaneity and violence. But it was difficult to plan on those terms when relying on people whose allegiance was doubtful. The idea of the Trojan horse is a good one, but it needs more reliable helpers inside the city walls than Vichy provided. As things turned out the rickety house of treacherous cards played by Darlan collapsed partly of its own frailty and partly of the added treachery of the Vichy Prime Minister, Laval, who invoked Hitler's aid directly and was given a vague promise of air support in Tunisia – when the Allies got there. There were, during the four days succeeding the invasion, orders to ceasefire, counterorders, arrests, sporadic fighting, frantic telephoning to the inadequate Pétain and a meeting between him and the American *chargé d'affaires* in Vichy. Pétain was given a message from Roosevelt pleading for cooperation and replied expressing 'bewilderment and sadness' at the American aggression. He might well have been bewildered. Less than a week previously he had received a letter from Roosevelt with the salutation 'My dear old friend.' He was 86 and his mind wandered in memories of Verdun in 1916. 'France will resist attacks on her

Left: Eisenhower with Darlan and Clark. Eisenhower's support of Darlan raised a storm of protest.

empire, even those that are made by old friends,' he told the Vichy *chargé d'affaires*. 'That is the order I give.' But whatever order he gave it was Darlan who decided the issue. After sending a message to Pétain on the afternoon of 8 November saying 'Algiers will probably be taken this evening' he received in reply a humble message of trust: 'You have my full confidence.' Two days later he sold out to Mark Clark and his treachery sealed the success of Torch.

Years later Eisenhower was to recall the despair he had felt while 'burrowed in a damp cave with dim lights in the rock of Gibraltar.' In recollection he was able to add a touch of humor, but at the time there was little but 'the wretched entanglement of politics,' which he hated. In the midst of the farcical crisscross of egotism, chicanery, and political blackmail there were few admirable qualities to be seen except the heroism of such as Captain Peters and the willing cooperation of the British in accepting American command. For the most part he seemed to be surrounded by men with whom he had to make deals that appeared to those who were not on the spot to be the gravest errors of judgment and morality. He had ratified Clark's deal with Darlan and in consequence faced a tremendous salvo of criticism from Britain and America alike. The critics included not only Ed Murrow, the London-based CBS radio commentator, who snapped out on the air that he did not know 'what the hell Eisenhower was about in sleeping with the Nazis,' but also Churchill himself. Part of the answer to Murrow's outburst could have been given by Roosevelt, who had seen a profitable tie-up between the Congressional elections and an American victory in North Africa; the rest could have been detected in Churchill's deviousness – a characteristic he managed to wrap up well in bombast and rhetoric. He had caused the church bells to be rung throughout Britain on 15 November to celebrate the Alamein and Torch victories (a grain of comfort he rightly thought Britain deserved after three years of major reverses) and two days later was heading off heavy Parliamentary criticism by telling Roosevelt (copy to Eisenhower) that 'Very deep currents of feeling are stirred by the arrangement with Darlan.' Eisenhower might well have pointed out

that the 'arrangement' to 'kiss Darlan's ass if necessary' had been the cornerstone of Churchill's bid for the French navy. He refrained from doing so, merely observing in a letter to his son John, 'From what I hear of what has been appearing in the newspapers, you are learning that it is easy enough for a man to be a newspaper hero one day and a bum the next. The answer is that just as one must not let his head get swelled too much by a bit of acclaim, he must not be too much irritated when the pack turns on him.'

The pack continued to turn for several weeks. There were many bitter references to 'the Eisenhower-Darlan cabal.' Numerous telegrams oscillated between the pro- and anti-Vichy factions. Increasing ire was shown by the people of both Britain and America toward a pact for which they could see no justification. Churchill and Roosevelt were forced to explain that the justification was military expediency, that the 'arrangement' was purely temporary, and that the French would be free to choose their own form of government once they had been 'liberated from the yoke of the common foe.' In London the word 'sellout' continued to be bruited abroad and Churchill had to seek the refuge of a Secret Session of the House of Commons. Explaining that since 1776 Britain had had no say in American policy, he added that Americans had no such reasons to despise Darlan as had England, and the fact that Generals Clark and Eisenhower had come to an arrangement with him had at least resulted in the Vichy French turning their arms

against the Axis forces and thereby aiding the Allied invasion. The grumbling voices of dissent were quietened and the press removed its claws from Churchill's back. But in the end silence was achieved – fortuitously – only by criminal means. On Christmas Eve, Darlan was shot by a fanatical young man named Bonnier de la Chapelle and died within the hour. The assassin was an ardent De Gaullist who imagined himself to be the savior of France; but his saving grace did him little good, for he was tried by court-martial and shot at dawn on 28 December. The Darlan episode was to all intents and purposes closed. Although in writing to his son Eisenhower had brushed its repercussions aside as one of the misfortunes of war, he had been deeply hurt by the snarls of 'Fascist' and 'Hitlerite' that had issued from press and radio. He told the Minister Resident at Allied Headquarters, Harold Macmillan, that he could not understand 'why these long-haired, starry-eyed guys keep gunning for me. I'm no reactionary. Christ on the mountain! I'm as idealistic as hell.'

Whatever his feelings, he was not the sort to brood upon them. In any case, with the closure of the Darlan episode (so far as Eisenhower was concerned with a letter of condolence to the sorrowing widow) and a ceasefire on the political front he was able to concentrate on 'real action at last.' The foothold in

Below: Kepner with Carl Spaatz of the Eighth USAF which transferred aircraft to North Africa for Torch.

North Africa gained by the Allies was satisfactory in its way but as Harry Butcher said in the diary, 'No more than the first step in kicking the Germans and Eyeties out of Africa.' The impetus of Montgomery's westward drive was being maintained and must be met by the eastward drive of the Torch forces. On the battleground of Tunisia the two arms of the pincer would meet and crush Rommel's Afrika Korps between them. That at any rate was the plan. Like all plans it was subject to the caprices of fortune; and for a time fortune favored the foe. General Anderson's Eastern Task Force had edged its way to the Tunisian border and had captured some minor objectives with the aid of paratroops, but was spread extremely thinly over the featureless brown land that was now swept by rain. The Axis had the tremendous advantage of holding airfields much closer to the fighting zone than those of the Allies, whose bombers had to take off from runways more than 100 miles away and were fuelled, maintained and replaced from Algiers, 300-miles distant. 'We have gone beyond the sustainable limit of air capabilities in supporting ground forces in a pell-mell race for Tunisia,' Eisenhower reported back to Churchill and the Chiefs of Staff on 3 December.

During November, while he was still entangled in politics, he had emerged from his headquarters in the Rock and flown off to the front. Though still constrained by the machinations of the statesmen he was overjoyed to be tactically involved. One of his objects was to assess the value of the French troops, who outnumbered the enemy but seemed to be ineffective. The reasons soon became clear. The men were cosmopolitan North Africans and temperamentally unsuited for active service. Such equipment as they had was antiquated and useless against tanks and aircraft; their transport relied on mules, their communications on the cleft stick and runner. There were no medical supplies, no stores of clothing and little rapport between the officers and the men because of language barriers. 'Of the sixteen to eighteen French battalions (so called),' Eisenhower wrote to Bedell Smith, 'I estimate that we may get a combat efficiency of about one battalion. The figure can easily go up if Giraud and Juin . . . can actually galvanize the

troops into serious effort. They will not be of any great use offensively but they could do a lot of protecting of our flanks and establishments in the rear.'

The bleakness of the scene was no more inspiring, with cactus, scrub, bogged-down tanks and vehicles half buried in the glutinous mud. 'Like the world before creation,' Eisenhower wrote to Mamie. But forward troops found his presence cheering. As Mark Clark observed in *Calculated Risk*, 'His clichés were ludicrously unfunny . . . but his Cheshire cat grin made them effective.' Also effective was his grasp of the tactical situation. Fox Connor had told him, 'Leave the theories of Leavenworth and the Point alone: adapt the eye and the ear and above all the personality to the battle in hand. Principles are sometimes best overthrown.' He could do nothing about the rain. Personality clashes he had always been good at handling and he listened patiently to Fredendall's bombastic Anglophobia finding its expression in sneering comments on Anderson's leadership. 'You're both good guys,' he told Fredendall. 'Pulling together is everything.' Fredendall could scarcely believe his ears. 'It was like an Andy Hardy film. I just waited for Judge Lewis Stone to stretch out the fatherly hand to bad boy Micky Rooney's shoulder. It was like a pep talk from the British Empire. Where the hell he mashed up such junk from I'll never know. It don't matter. You just listen to the guy in amazement. And you find you're with him because he's slipped you a chance to have a snicker at him first.' Like a writer of romantic fiction, Eisenhower managed to keep his tongue out of his cheek long enough to blind people with sincerity. 'Soothing syrup has its uses,' he observed to Harry Butcher. As for principles, there were none to be overthrown in Tunisia – anyway not for the time being. The task was simply to get as many troops forward as could be transported and maintained, plus the support of ever-increasing numbers of bombers. The lack of air support, and of a single experienced coordinating commander for bombers, fighters and transport planes, worried him considerably. There was just such a man, Air Marshal Sir Arthur Tedder, who was dedicated to the proposition that air supremacy was more important than either land or sea operations or any

combination of them. He had enormously aided Montgomery's success at El Alamein and had, as Eisenhower was quick to observe, 'exactly the kind of experience and leadership' needed for the Tunis situation. But Torch had its own air commander, General Carl Spaatz of the Eighth USAF, and Eisenhower was reluctant, as he put it to Bedell Smith, 'to have myself any more troubles around the personality area.' Tedder, however, remained foremost in his

thoughts of reorganization.

Meanwhile the rain poured down. The close proximity of the German airfields gave the enemy the advantage despite the Allies' numerical superiority, and although in Eisenhower's opinion Anderson had 'worked like a dog and . . . has done everything . . . humanly possible to make the big gamble win,' no commander could maneuver his forces over ground continually being churned into a morass. With an optimism that turned out to be misplaced Eisenhower called the attack – which in the circumstances was an attack in name only – to a halt and conferred with Anderson about regrouping and renewing the attack 'in ten days or a couple of weeks when the weather breaks.' As had happened many times in the history of warfare, the weather had proved a factor far more decisive than strategy, men or arms.

'Yet,' as the historian Liddell Hart points out, 'by the irony of luck, this failure turned out to be one of the biggest blessings in disguise that could have happened. For without such a failure Hitler and Mussolini would not have had the time and encouragement to pour very large reinforcements into Tunisia and build up the defense of that bridgehead to a strength of over a

Below: At the Casablanca Conference in 1943 it was decided to invade Italy once Operation Torch was complete.

quarter of a million men – who had to fight with an enemy-dominated sea at their back, and if defeated would be trapped.' Upon those words 'if defeated' hung the fate not only of the Tunisian campaign but also of the mighty Overlord.

Liddell Hart was of course writing with hindsight. Eisenhower had only his cheery optimism when he ordered a short respite before regrouping to allow the weather to break. In the event the weather did not break. This might have been expected. The unvarying local pattern was for a rainy season of six months, but the pattern seems to have been ignored by everyone except Eisenhower, who was to remember the lesson on 5 June 1944. Hitler's new commander in the African campaign, Colonel General Jurgen von Arnim, set about expanding the Axis bridgehead with his Fifth Panzer Army and the mighty new Tiger tank, whose weaknesses had not yet been discovered. About this 56-ton leviathan Eisenhower said to Patton, 'Who would have dreamed of our baby growing into such a big boy?' The formidable Tiger was brought into the bridgehead by rail and used sparingly while the weather was bad; but Carl Spaatz's Intelligence branch did not lack news of the concentration of armor near the enemy's all-weather airfields from which flights of fighters took off like birds from a harvested cornfield whenever his bombers, severely frustrated by an ever-lengthening supply line, warily approached. Eisenhower and Tedder met and the Supreme Commander went through the bureaucratic protocols and applied to the Chiefs of Staff for the loan of Tedder as an adviser. The request was turned down. Alan Brooke thought the request a frivolous one, part of Eisenhower's buffoonery and acidly pointed out that Tedder was already air commander in chief, Middle East, and was hardly to be called upon in an 'advisory' capacity. 'With your approval,' his reply said with heavy sarcasm, 'Tedder can take over complete responsibility for all air operations in North Africa.' Eisenhower refused to be put out over the slight to his, and Spaatz's, efficiency and pointed

Right: Left to right around Churchill are Eden, Brooke, Tedder, Cunningham, Alexander, Marshall, Eisenhower and Montgomery.

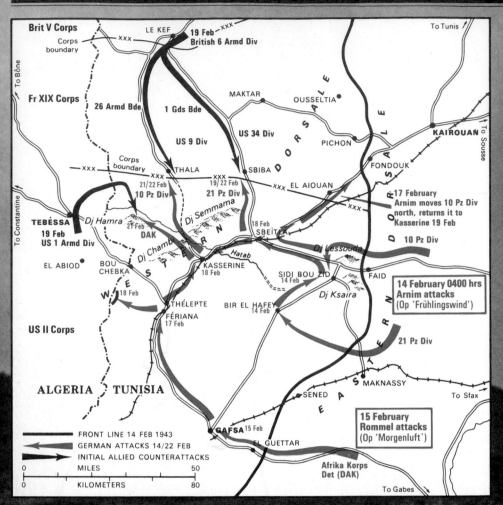

On the map:

Brit V Corps
Corps boundary
LE KEF — 19 Feb — **British 6 Armd Div**

To Tunis

To Bône

Fr XIX Corps

26 Armd Bde

1 Gds Bde

MAKTAR

OUSSELTIA

DORSALE

US 9 Div

US 34 Div

PICHON

KAIROUAN

To Sousse

Corps boundary

THALA

SBIBA

EL AIOUAN

FONDOUK

17 February
Arnim moves 10 Pz Div north, returns it to Kasserine 19 Feb

21/22 Feb
10 Pz Div

19/22 Feb
21 Pz Div

To Constantine

TEBÉSSA
19 Feb
US 1 Armd Div

Dj Hamra
21 Feb

Dj Semmama

DAK

18 Feb
SBEÏTLA

10 Pz Div

EL ABIOD

Dj Chamb...

KASSERINE
18 Feb

Hatab

Dj Lessouda

FAID

BOU CHEBKA

SIDI BOU ZID
14 Feb

Dj Ksaira

**14 February 0400 hrs
Arnim attacks
(Op 'Frühlingswind')**

18 Feb

THÉLEPTE
FÉRIANA
17 Feb

BIR EL HAFEY
14 Feb

21 Pz Div

US II Corps

MAKNASSY

To Sfax

ALGERIA — TUNISIA

SENED

GAFSA 15 Feb
EL GUETTAR

**15 February
Rommel attacks
(Op 'Morgenluft')**

FRONT LINE 14 FEB 1943
GERMAN ATTACKS 14/22 FEB
INITIAL ALLIED COUNTERATTACKS

0   MILES   50
0   KILOMETERS   80

Afrika Korps
Det (DAK)

To Gabes

out that Tedder could not be expected to serve Alexander and Montgomery in one area and himself in another with totally different tactical problems. The matter was dropped for the time being, but the delicacy of the situation did not go unrecorded:

High command, particularly Allied Command, in war carries with it a lot of things that were never included in our text books, in the Leavenworth course, or even in the War College investigation. I think sometimes that I am a cross between a one timer soldier, a pseudo-statesman, a jack-legged politician and a crooked diplomat. I walk a soapy tightrope in a rainstorm with a blazing furnace on

Left: The Battle for Kasserine.

Below: US antitank gunners in Kasserine.

one side and a pack of ravenous tigers on the other.

While Eisenhower saw his 10-day respite lengthening into weeks, the statesmen again went into conclave with their Chiefs of Staff. This time the venue was Casablanca. Stalin was unable to get there because of more pressing matters in Moscow, where he was directing the tremendous battle for the recovery of Stalingrad, now reaching its climax; but Roosevelt and Churchill forgathered on 16 January 1943 to work out their aims. Eisenhower and Alexander attended the conference and De Gaulle was invited over from London to make his peace with Giraud, which he did without much enthusiasm. Giraud had been appointed High Commissioner in North Africa as a consolation prize for having accepted Eisenhower's supreme command in the Torch operation and

continued to portray himself as a glamorous figure beloved by the multitude; but Mark Clark had been right in saying that his pulling power was virtually nil. It was De Gaulle's personality that the multitudes of the Resistance fell for; and, the Resistance being by definition an underground movement, nothing much of its furtive machinations was seen on the surface. Its tentacles, unhampered now by Darlan and his Vichy adherents, reached throughout France and captured the allegiance of thousands. 'The President,' Eisenhower wrote, 'can hardly be expected to be pleased. De Gaulle acts like a Prima Donna, a spoilt kid sulking because he can't get the flavor icecream he wants.' The French leader's arrogance did not please Churchill either. He threatened to topple De Gaulle from his perch as the leader of a Free French Movement supported by the Allies if he did not cooperate.

De Gaulle unsmilingly inclined his haughty head a degree or two and went to see Roosevelt; but there was no accord between them – only an icy formality and an acknowledgment by the President that De Gaulle had a 'spiritual look in his eyes.' Whatever it was, it aroused the enthusiasm of the motley crew of French soldiers in North Africa to a far higher level than Giraud had achieved. Eisenhower wrote again to Bedell Smith and told him that there had been much improvement since November. 'We can use these troops usefully, so we've got to keep the right side of De Gaulle for the next move.'

The next move was a matter for great argument. Italy, the weakest of the Axis foes, could be vanquished with advantage to the Mediterranean shipping situation; but where should the attack be made? Sardinia or Sicily? Roosevelt did not really care which so long as the job

Special Order of the Day

HEADQUARTERS
18th ARMY GROUP
21st April, 1943

SOLDIERS OF THE ALLIES

1. Two months ago, when the Germans and Italians were attacking us, I told you that if you held firm, final victory was assured.

2. You did your duty and now you are about to reap its full reward.

3. We have reached the last phase of this campaign. We have grouped our victorious Armies and are going to drive the enemy into the sea.

   We have got them just where we want them—with their backs to the wall.

4. This final battle will be fierce, bitter and long, and will demand all the skill, strength and endurance of each one of us.

   But you have proved yourselves the masters of the battle-field, and therefore you will win this last great battle which will give us the whole of North Africa.

5. The eyes of the world are on you—and the hopes of all at home.

FORWARD THEN, TO VICTORY

H. R. Alexander

General,

Commander, 18th Army Group

Above: The Special Order of the Day issued by General Alexander before the final attack on Tunis.

could be done quickly and the combined forces of the Allies concentrated on the full-scale second front invasion of northern France. Eisenhower was equally indifferent. His mind was on the continuation of the battle to squeeze the Axis forces out of Africa. He had a recurrence of the feeling of frustration that always affected him when he was in the midst of the wranglings of politicians and sought comfort from his chauffeuse Kay Summersby. Putting the words 'Supreme Commander' in mocking quotes he added, 'It's a laugh.' But he was mollified when as a result of a Chiefs of Staff decision at Casablanca there was a reorganization and he was given command of a new Army Group, the 18th, which comprised both Anderson's First Army and Montgomery's Eighth. Alexander was appointed his deputy as Supreme Commander and Mark Clark was given a corps command.

Eisenhower could thus shelve the Sicily-Sardinia problem for the time being and concentrate on reopening the battle for Tunis. This he did with the fourth star of a full general on his epaulettes. His promotion to the highest rank in the United States army had been promulgated on 11 February 1943.

Montgomery's forces captured Tripoli on 23 January and the German surrender of Stalingrad came eight days later. It was the first outright and ignominious defeat of any of Hitler's armies. Nearly 100,000 men of Paulus's Sixth Army went into captivity and twice that number had died in the battle for the city. 'The God of War has gone over to the other side,' the Führer said – with perspicacity as it turned out.

February saw the break in the weather Eisenhower had been waiting for. The rain gave way to violent sandstorms which were equally unpleasant but not

so harassing to movement. Rommel and Von Arnim were at loggerheads over the use of a Panzer division and a day was wasted while their cross-purposes were untangled; Anderson and Fredendall, planning to hold the Germans at the Kasserine Pass, managed to cooperate with each other to the extent of making a successful stand at Sbiba. It was during this and the preceding and subsequent skirmishes that Eisenhower saw the weaknesses in command and decided on changes. Intelligence was a weakness in First Army and he replaced the then-encumbent of the office of Chief with Brigadier Kenneth Strong, a man of many languages and wide experience who was to remain Eisenhower's eyes and ears with regard to enemy movements until 1945. Lloyd Fredendall was also troublesome because of his aggressiveness toward subordinates and because his grasp of tactics was not equal to commanding a corps. Typically, Eisenhower did not bother about going into the reasons for his Anglophobia or his emotional immaturity. In a note to Marshall in Washington he said that Fredendall had 'many splendid abilities that should not be lost sight of.' Clearly Eisenhower wanted to lose sight of them as soon as possible. He replaced them with the very different abilities of George Patton, whose 'blood-and-guts' flamboyance Fredendall had unsuccessfully tried to emulate. Patton took over II Corps and Eisenhower gave him Omar Bradley as his second in command. 'There will be no more hesitation, no more defensive tactics when attack is needed.' One would think not indeed. Patton had under his command four divisions with a total strength of 88,000 men and fewer than 6000 Axis forces in opposition; for Rommel and Arnim had for months been far inferior in strength to the Allies. It was simply by careful maneuver that they managed to make the most of them – a skill that Eisenhower was well aware the inexperienced American forces lacked. The British forces did not lack experience, but their leadership was often at fault. Though seemingly not given to hesitation, Montgomery often failed to exploit his victories, while the rule-book pauses for regrouping made by Anderson and Alexander were welcomed by Rommel for the opportunities they gave him to send in short sharp sorties that could commit damage quite disproportionate to their size. 'They're too damn gentlemanly, these British,' Eisenhower said.

Tunisia was Eisenhower's first essay in command of large forces. It was obvious that his greatest attribute as a commander was his ability to delegate. Next came his conscientiousness toward the units at the front of the battle. His visits forward equalled those of Montgomery in informality and frequency; but they were never made to merely cheer up the troops. He was encouraging but he never failed to point to weaknesses in discipline, shortcomings in performance and errors in tactics that could have been avoided with 'more positive thinking.' He was a salesman of the art of war who put over his product in terms of Dale Carnegie platitudes and got away with it. He modestly told Harry Butcher to remind him that in the regular army he was only a Lieutenant Colonel, and that only the war had taken him to generalship. 'All the same,'

Butcher recorded, 'backwoodsman he might be, but the extent of his command never overwhelmed him as it might have done a more actively experienced man.' It did indeed astonish Eisenhower to think that, except for 'that great fellow Archie Wavell' he was the first commander in history with responsibility for land, sea and air forces; 'and Archie's spell didn't last long.' However, it seemed to him a natural form of command, 'for the proper integration of the three arms calls for a single director.'

The battles in Tunisia dragged on until May, while more and more combat troops and more and more guns and tanks arrived until in the end the Axis forces were stupefyingly outnumbered. Rommel, a sick man, returned to Europe and told Hitler that unless the German forces withdrew from Africa they would make their graves there – 'They are being stamped into the ground by Americans.' Hitler went through the motions of sympathy then told the great

'Desert Fox,' for whose skill and bravery even foes had the greatest admiration, that he had lost his nerve. Rommel did not deign to reply, and Hitler, aware that he had gone too far, added consolingly, 'You must get fit again quickly, for soon you will be in command of operations to recover Casablanca.' No plans to recover Casablanca ever existed except in Hitler's mind, and even there must have had a very tenuous lodging, for the Führer was only too well aware that he was outnumbered in the air, on the ground and at sea. He was particularly outnumbered at sea as the French fleet, for so long the rich prize on which both Allies and Axis had cast covetous eyes, had remained anchored in Toulon until 27 November 1942, when it was scuttled at the very moment the Germans were about to lay hands on it; and the Italian

Below: General Auchinleck heads a conference of Middle East Chiefs, 29 March 1942.

Above: Eisenhower in North Africa in 1943.

Left: Patton and Eisenhower met for a conference near Tunisia, after which Eisenhower pinned three stars on General Patton.

navy, falling victim to Cunningham's Mediterranean Fleet, had faded to the proportions of a toy armada. Specifically, the balance of power in April was divided thus: there were 300,000 Allied troops in the field amply provided with artillery and tanks (some 1500 tanks); Flying Fortress bombers and Mustang fighters had wrenched command of the air from Göring's Luftwaffe; and the Axis ground forces had diminished to fewer than 60,000 combat troops and 100 tanks. There is no doubt that even that shrunken army would have put up a formidable opposition had it not been starved of supplies; but Eisenhower had wisely directed that 'the blockade should be used like a thumbscrew to make the enemy squeal' and it had had its inevitable effect. On the morning of 9 May General von Vaerst of Fifth Panzer Army sent a message to Arnim: 'Our armor and artillery have been destroyed. Without ammunition and fuel. We shall fight to the last.' By midday the time had come for surrender. Four days later Churchill received a telegram from General Alexander: 'Sir: It is my duty to report that the Tunisian campaign is over. All enemy resistance has ceased. We are masters of the North African shores.' Churchill was rewarded with a telegram from the King:

'Now that the campaign in Africa has reached a glorious conclusion, I wish to tell you how profoundly I appreciate the fact that its initial conception and successful prosecution are largely due to your vision and to your unflinching determination in the face of early difficulties. The African campaign has immeasurably increased the debt that this country, and indeed all the United Nations, owe to you. GEORGE R.I.'

Eisenhower received no telegram but a personal visit from the King. In June George VI paid a visit to the troops in North Africa, gave a dinner for the commanders, and invested Eisenhower with the KCB – the Knight Grand Cross Commander of the Most Honorable Order of the Bath.

5: IFS, BUTS, MIGHTS

'In London,' Churchill recorded, 'there was for the first time a real lifting of the spirits.' Such a lifting of the spirits was richly deserved by forces and populace alike; but it was not fully shared by Eisenhower. It is evident from his letters and diaries of that time that it bothered him that such enormous Allied efforts had been necessary to overcome no more than four German divisions. Also, he seems to have been conscious of some failure on his own part as Supreme Commander to fight 'according to the book': 'I think the best way to describe our operations to date is that they have violated every recognized principle of war, are in conflict with all operational and logistic methods laid down in textbooks, and will be condemned in their entirety by all Leavenworth and War College classes for the next twenty-five years.'

Nevertheless a major victory had been scored and the next step now had to be decided. Another conference – this time called Trident – was arranged and Churchill arrived in Washington on 12 May, having crossed the Atlantic in the *Queen Mary*. It amused him to write to Mrs Churchill and tell her that 'in the

holds there were 5,000 German prisoners to keep me company.'

For once there was no profitless argument about the next step. It was agreed that the best way of taking the weight off the Eastern Front, where 185 German divisions were still engaged, would be to knock Italy out of the war. Some of those German divisions would then perforce be withdrawn to hold down the Balkans – if contact could be made with Yugoslavia and Turkey brought into the war on the Allied side. A good many possible problems were hazily seen but neither Roosevelt, Churchill, nor the Chiefs of Staff came properly to terms with them. They seemed to be gripped by the euphoria of their victory, determined only on fixing a time and place for the next step.

Sicily was the chosen objective, 10 July the launching date for the invasion,

Right: Eisenhower and Gort inspect the guard of honor at Vedalla Palace, Malta.

Below: Eisenhower just before being presented the Grand Cross of the Legion of Honor by Giraud.

which was to have the codename Husky. Eisenhower was again appointed Supreme Commander, this time with Alexander, who was senior in both rank and experience, as his deputy. In that appointment the historian Liddell Hart saw 'significant acceptance of the United States as the senior partner in the alliance,' and this despite the fact that not only was Eisenhower junior in status but there would also be a preponderance of British forces. Montgomery and Patton were appointed the commanders of the two invading armies, Cunningham continued to be in command at sea, and to Eisenhower's delight he had Tedder as Commander in Chief of Mediterranean Air Command.

A famous subterfuge was used to mislead Hitler into believing that the invasion would be launched against Sardinia and Greece. This was concocted by British Intelligence, who arranged for the body of a supposed British officer to be washed ashore on the Spanish coast and to fall into the hands of Nazi agents. On the body had been planted documents convincingly designed to show that preparations for the landings in Sicily were a cover up and that the real objectives were Sardinia and Greece. The Germans were completely fooled. Hitler immediately ordered the 1st Panzer Division and the 90th Panzergrenadier Division into Sardinia and the

Below: Tedder was Commander in Chief of air forces under Eisenhower for the Italian Campaign.

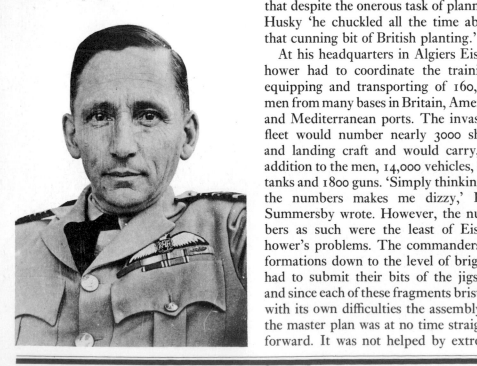

11th Air Corps to the south of France, ready to counter the expected Allied landings. Eisenhower evidently took a childlike delight in the way the High Command was fooled. Butcher records that despite the onerous task of planning Husky 'he chuckled all the time about that cunning bit of British planting.'

At his headquarters in Algiers Eisenhower had to coordinate the training, equipping and transporting of 160,000 men from many bases in Britain, America and Mediterranean ports. The invasion fleet would number nearly 3000 ships and landing craft and would carry, in addition to the men, 14,000 vehicles, 600 tanks and 1800 guns. 'Simply thinking of the numbers makes me dizzy,' Kay Summersby wrote. However, the numbers as such were the least of Eisenhower's problems. The commanders of formations down to the level of brigade had to submit their bits of the jigsaw, and since each of these fragments bristled with its own difficulties the assembly of the master plan was at no time straightforward. It was not helped by extreme

Above: Eisenhower reviews WAACs in North Africa just prior to the start of the Sicilian Campaign.

differences of temperament between Patton and Montgomery. 'George has no love of the British in general or of Monty in particular,' Eisenhower noted. 'They're like oil and water to each other. Monty has lofty ideas about G.Is' "inexperience" and Harold [Alexander] doesn't help with his gentlemanly arrogance. These character problems aren't likely to lessen.' As would be seen, he was only too right.

As if such complexities were not enough, Eisenhower was given yet another political clash to subdue by diplomacy. The two French Generals, De Gaulle and Giraud, were still acting like prima donnas despite the outward show of conciliation they had demonstrated at Casablanca in January. Churchill had unwisely attempted to found an association called the French Committee of National Liberation with joint presidents De Gaulle and Giraud. Its purpose was to ease Allied cooperation with the French armed forces in whatever theater they might be. After the third meeting of this ill-conceived enterprise De Gaulle had huffily withdrawn because neither he nor Giraud could agree about which of them would control the French army – Giraud wanting only military control, De Gaulle seeing himself as combining the qualities of a political and military genius with the future of France in his hands alone. Not surprisingly considering his lack of fondness for De Gaulle, Roosevelt would have been happy to see the back of him. The unprejudiced Eisenhower saw things from a more balanced viewpoint, put that viewpoint to the President by way of Bedell Smith, and was rewarded with the task of 'sorting out the roles of the two Prima Donnas.'

He invited them to join him for talks on 19 July. 'Only my Chief of Staff [Bedell Smith] will join us, so there will be no outside influences.' Nor were there. Eisenhower and Bedell Smith, both acting with the utmost restraint and diplomacy, convinced the two Frenchmen that the Allies' continued success depended on their complete cooperation. De Gaulle climbed down to the extent of agreeing to Giraud keeping control of the army in exchange for a guarantee that there would be no British or American interference in the political future of France. However, Eisenhower was under no delusions as to the permanent closure of the rift. 'You can marry them, but whether they will stay married is another thing altogether' he observed to Harry Butcher; and his doubts proved to be right. Within a few months the two Generals were indulging in another bout of malicious sulks from which Giraud emerged defeated and soon faded into insignificance both militarily and politically. But for the time being Eisenhower's gift for harmonizing discordant personalities was entirely successful in securing his object, which was to be untrammelled by French bickering while Operation Husky was going on. It must not be forgotten, either, that he not only wanted to be liked but also wanted to be seen to justify admiration. It pleased him to be called – as he had been by Roosevelt – 'a master of psychological diplomacy.'

The invasion of Sicily had begun on 10 July with Montgomery's Eighth Army attacking the southeast corner of the island and Patton's United States Seventh Army making a four-pronged landing at points west from Agrigento to Gela. Eisenhower, having pulled all the threads of his command together, went to his new invasion headquarters in Malta and gave the signal for the invasion to be launched in the early hours of the 10th, despite adverse weather conditions which hindered the paratroops' landings but put the defenders at a disadvantage because they were surprised by landings made in stormy weather. The forces used were enormous – even bigger than those to be used in Overlord in June 1944, with more than 1000 aircraft taking part; nevertheless, not all went well.

The plan had been for the Eighth Army to advance rapidly north to Messina and cut off the escape route of the Axis forces across the strait, while Patton's Seventh Army drove them into Montgomery's arms. In the event things did not turn out as planned. The commander of the German airborne troops, General Student, proposed an immediate airborne counterattack on the Allied landings; but this was turned down by Hitler, who still believed that Sicily was a feint. Student was restricted to sending a parachute division to reinforce the sparse German troops in the Catania area. Some of the paratroopers landed almost simultaneously with their British opponents in the area of the bridge over the Simeto river. There ensued a fierce battle for the bridge which the British paratroopers lost and did not recapture for three days, after a rescue operation by Montgomery's main ground troops. The delay allowed the buildup of German and Italian reserves to oppose the British strike straight across Sicily to Messina. Montgomery now had to divert his

Below: Eisenhower during a visit to Malta to discuss plans with high-ranking army and navy officials.

Above: A Bren-gun carrier comes ashore at Sicily. Eisenhower was Supreme Commander of the operation.

forces to the hilly country round Mount Etna, where he was held up still further by the difficult terrain. This gave Patton a chance to detach himself from the rôle of protector of Montgomery's flank and make a whirlwind advance to Messina, which he reached with typical drama – but not before the Axis forces had made an orderly escape across the Strait and into the toe of Italy. 'As I had foreseen and warned Ike,' said Alexander, 'the object of the exercise was frustrated by his vetoing my plan for landings in the north as well as the south.'

In the end, it did not make a lot of difference. The conquest of Sicily was achieved in under six weeks – 'Only,' as Eisenhower wryly observed, 'to be treated as another political issue.'

That was true. The Chiefs of Staff urged the seizing of the advantage afforded by Italy's impending economic collapse to impose terms of surrender that would simply wipe out the Italian forces' nuisance value. But the politicians – British and American – would have

Right: Paratroopers board their C-47 Dakota transports in Tunisia for the invasion of Sicily.

none of it. They wanted a grandiloquent document that covered every aspect of an unconditional surrender. This took weeks to compile in suitably statesman-like language. During that time Mussolini was dismissed and General Badoglio appointed his successor; Rommel was given command of eight German divisions to resist Allied invasion of the Italian mainland; Fascist leaders fled; and Badoglio unsuccessfully attempted a political double-cross that he somewhat oddly thought would leave Italy poised in a friendly vacuum between Hitler and the Allies.

On a lower level another difficult situation developed and extended Eisenhower's powers of diplomacy to their utmost. Not surprisingly, it had to do with Patton, who combined not only an immaculate appearance with blood-and-guts bravery but also an almost revivalist devotion to hymn singing and praying

with a blasphemous line in oaths. 'I'm the best goddam butt-kicker in the whole United States army' was his boast. As well he may have been, and would have been welcomed as such so long as he kept the boast in the field of braggadocio. But implementing the boast to the humiliation of others was too much – particularly in a field hospital. He had been talking with seriously wounded and dying soldiers during the campaign in Sicily and had encountered a whimpering Pfc suffering from severe battle shock. His whimpering enraged Patton, who yelled at the boy 'You gutless bastard' and slapped him round the face with his leather gloves. Naturally the hospital staff reported the incident to the senior medical officer, who in turn added a red-ink rider to his daily report to the Director of Medical Services. Two days later a similar incident occurred at another field hospital. This time

Patton reached for one of his famous pearl-handled pistols and threatened to shoot the cowering soldier or have him put in front of a firing squad. 'I ought to shoot you myself, you goddammed sniveling coward!' Patton might have got away with a severe reprimand for one incident; but two at such a short interval could have meant a court martial and the end of his army career. Eisenhower thought about the problem for an hour and came to the conclusion that the United States army could not afford to lose Patton, but that the offense must be punished with humiliation of a degree equal to that inflicted. For the record, Patton's personal file had a reprimand entered but, much more wounding to his pride, he was ordered to apologize

Below: Eisenhower pictured at a meeting with some of his Chiefs of Staff for the Sicilian Campaign.

personally to the soldiers he had insulted and to the hospitals and staffs concerned. He also had to address representative groups of all the units of Seventh Army and tell them that he had acted on impulse and that no reflection on their fighting spirit had been intended. He did it with style, his recorded words being 'I thought I'd stand up here and let you fellers see if I'm as big a sonofabitch as you think I am.'

The war correspondents who went everywhere with the army naturally got hold of the story, and Eisenhower wisely did not attempt to suppress it by so much as a single detail. He simply told the press that to release the story at the moment might hamper the war effort, while to hold it for release at a more suitable time could add to its drama. He did nothing beyond that to influence the press one way or the other, leaving it entirely to their own judgment. The story did not appear for some three months, and when it did every detail was reported – including the description of Patton's personal tank painted in red, white and blue, and the origin of the 'Blood-and-guts' sobriquet. That had come from the introductory talk he gave to officer cadets: 'War is a killing busi-

Below: Waco CG-4 gliders being prepared in Sicily to reinforce the Salerno beachhead on 13 September 1943.

ness. You've gotta spill their blood or they'll spill yours. Rip 'em up the belly or shoot 'em in the guts.' To emphasize points in the talk he used a saber he had himself designed with deep grooves for the extra speedy draining away of the victim's blood. Eisenhower was not unpleased with his own performance in his handling of the situation. 'Tricky,' he told Butcher, 'But I guess I understand what made George loose off his mouth: he saw a reflection of his real self in those shot-up boys.' His instinct for understanding the other man's point of view was revealed in that sentence; but it was one of the few occasions when he gave it expression.

Meanwhile, back on the battlefield of Italy, the fruit of the politicians' wranglings had resulted in an effort to get Italy to surrender without further conflict. The Allies had supposed that Badoglio and the King, Victor Emanuel III, could extricate themselves from the Führer's influence now that Mussolini had been banished to the island of Ponza and make a separate peace. But it did not turn out that way. Mussolini had become the most hated man in Italy because as a consequence of his two decades of Fascist rule Italy found itself in a state of economic and military collapse. To soothe the populace Eisenhower was given something to read over the Italian radio. It had been written by the United States

Chiefs of Staff and said, in part: 'Your men will return to their normal life and their productive avocations, and hundreds of thousands of Italian prisoners now in our hands will return to the countless Italian homes who long for them. The ancient liberties and traditions of your country will be restored.' Fine words do not necessarily gain fine responses. They did not in this case which was not surprising. The country was still being tyrannized by Nazism, which was a more intensive version of the load it was trying to shed.

Neither Eisenhower nor the heads of state emerged with particular glory from the campaign in Italy. A form of surrender was signed by Badoglio's representative and Bedell Smith, representing Eisenhower on 3 September 1943. It contained the proviso that there should be a strong airborne landing in Rome to give the impression that the Italian forces there had been overcome despite strong efforts to fight back. 'They [the Italians] are dead scared that Hitler will put the whole weight of his fury on them if they don't make a show of fighting back,' Eisenhower wrote. He agreed to the airborne landing and then cancelled it, leaving loose ends everywhere and an impression of weakness which was smartly picked up by the Soviet government, whose interest in Italian affairs had been aroused by the

Right: C-47 Dakota transports prepare to take off for Salerno with reinforcement troops.

fact that the reaction to Fascism had brought about the growing strength of Communism. The Russians were treated peremptorily by the Anglo-American Control Commission that took over the authority of Italian government once the Eisenhower-Badoglio terms had been agreed. They were not given any say in the affairs of defeated Italy except at the remote level of the Advisory Council – an error the Allies were to regret, for the Russians were uncooperative when Allied interest was expressed in the Balkans – a not unimportant factor, for as Eisenhower noted, 'As in the first war Churchill is convinced that the back door to Germany opens through the Balkans.'

The Americans parted company from Churchill on that issue, as on many others. They had all along been half-hearted about the invasion of Italy and would have been much happier to withdraw the United States armies altogether and get them prepared for the big cross-channel invasion; but Roosevelt and the US Chiefs of Staff had cooperated with Churchill in exchange for a guarantee that American troops would be used only 'to tie the Germans down and thus prevent them from

assembling large-scale defense forces in France where the big hit was coming.' Any such guarantee was bound to rob the Italian campaign of the necessary lifeblood of enthusiasm; and indeed it was to drag on throughout the autumn and winter, with Eisenhower complaining to Marshall in Washington that he was 'bugged like a blue-assed fly, hamstrung by the politicians, while the Germans rustle up their forces and

prepare the defenses.'

At the very moment when Eisenhower was cancelling the airborne attack on Rome, General Mark Clark's Fifth Army, under Alexander's overall command, was nearing Salerno. It was the early hours of 9 September. The convoy had been seen approaching and the 16th Panzer Division had been alerted. It was a first-rate division and its task was to prevent Clark establishing a bridgehead before

Montgomery's Eighth Army had time to arrive from Calabria and add its weight. It almost succeeded. The fighting on the beaches was so fierce that Clark considered reembarking. That he did not do so was solely due to Admiral Cunningham's vehement protests, and the Fifth Army distinguished itself in nine days' fighting that firmly established the bridgehead. But it is doubtful if it could have held its ground without the support of such strategic bombers as Tedder was able to call into service, and the devastating effects of Royal Navy shelling. One German commander reported to Kesselring, 'The attack this morning came from at least sixteen to eighteen battle-

Below: A wounded GI is carried to a landing craft. The Germans inflicted heavy losses.

ships, cruisers, and big destroyers . . . with astonishing precision these ships shot at every recognized target with overwhelming effect.'

Cunningham's overwhelming effect had been achieved with 11,000 tons of shells aimed with remarkable accuracy. The air force's tonnage of bombs was considerably less – about 3000 – but that was due to Eisenhower's inability to

convince the Combined Chiefs of Staff of the urgency of his priority. He had foreseen that the success of the Salerno landing would depend largely on air support and as long ago as July had asked for four groups of Flying Fortresses to be

Right: Men of the 143rd Infantry come ashore, their task made more difficult by having no softening-up bombardment.

designated for the Mediterranean area. He had also pleaded for the retention of three groups of medium bombers, already in the area, to assist in the air attack. Both requests were refused with the excuse that the bomber offensive against German cities and industries was of prior importance. So the results gained by the forces actually available at Salerno were in no sense inconsiderable.

By 15 September the Fifth and Eighth Armies had linked up southeast of Salerno and Kesselring saw the wisdom of withdrawal before his forces were cut off. He ordered a strategic disengagement and prepared to fight again. Ironically, as soon as the success of the Salerno invasion had been firmly established the Combined Chiefs of Staff sent fulsome offers of further air support. 'Ask for anything you want,' Churchill cabled. It was a bitter thought that Clark's casualties, 14,000, would have been considerably fewer had Tedder had the bombers he needed for air assault. Eisenhower talked with Bedell Smith about the possibility of sending a message of sarcastic reproach, but thought better of it. Instead, he said in a return cable that the crisis was over but that he could certainly use some bombers to attack German lines of communication in northern Italy. These were supplied immediately.

Initial success having been achieved at

Below: Eisenhower (left), Lucas, and Clark leaving the War Room of 3rd Division after a conference.

Above: Field Marshal Smuts of South Africa visits Alexander and Eisenhower at advance AFHQ.

such great cost it would have been encouraging if the battle to get the Germans out of Italy had gone ahead with speed and panache. The capture of Rome would have meant great political prestige, and the airfields round the capital would have been invaluable.

On paper there seemed to be few obstacles. It was known through Intelligence that Hitler's plan had been to withdraw his forces to northern Italy and make a stand there. A fast drive up the leg of Italy, plus coordinated amphibious landings, was clearly the answer. Unfortunately, what was not known was that Kesselring had convinced the Führer that after remustering and

strengthening his forces he could mount a counteroffensive and, with any luck, drive the Allies 'back into the sea.' If a line could be held, say a hundred miles south of Rome, where the terrain, mountainous and riddled with waterways, was ideal for defense, the buildup for the counterattack could be prepared. Hitler agreed.

So it was at that stage that the Allied advance, which at the beginning of October had reached Naples and Foggia, got bogged down. Subsequent progress was slow and costly and was not helped by indecision among the Chiefs of Staff. The CIGS, Sir Alan Brooke, was particularly worried on this score, noting in his diary on 25 October that operations in Italy having come to a standstill it would be necessary to have 'an almighty row' with the Americans. He felt that

their halfheartedness about the Italian campaign was now beginning to have its effect, that their sole anxiety was to withdraw from Italy and get on with planning for the climatic cross-channel invasion. But as he rightly observed, Italy and Overlord interlocked; the first could not be abandoned without affecting the main issue.

With everything in a melting pot of indecision it was not surprising that Eisenhower found his task disheartening. 'Ifs, buts, mights,' he said to Kay Summersby. 'The British believe that *if* maximum forces can be applied in the Mediterranean, and *if* Russia can continue her present advances, and *if* the air offensive [on the Ruhr, Hamburg, and Berlin] continues successfully, we'll all be home in time for Thanksgiving. The only thing is, they don't say which year.'

6: THE LONG MARCH

Eisenhower's approach to all problems was, first, to have them cut down to size. However complex a situation, he wanted to see its essentials. His staff were frequently required to present in a few paragraphs on a single sheet of paper what he called 'the essence of a brew of troubles.' 'Peel away the fat and you get to the guts' was another of his picturesque phrases. Montgomery once referred to this characteristic as simplemindedness rather than clarity of vision. Hearing this, Eisenhower responded with the usual wide grin, 'The simple-minded are the special care of the Lord,' he said.

That may well be; but Eisenhower did not find the Lord or anyone else assisting him during the later days of the Italian campaign. Nor did it seem possible to avoid the mounting complexities toward which he was least sympathetic – the political. These complexities were irreducible to simplicity and Eisenhower found them getting under his skin to an extent that surprised and alarmed those

accustomed to his cheery outgoing nature. Harold Macmillan, the Minister Resident at Allied Forces headquarters, said he had never seen 'poor Eisenhower . . . so harassed' but did not wonder when he considered the conflicting orders that poured in upon him 'from the following sources: the Combined Chiefs of Staff, his official masters; General Marshall, Chief of the U.S. Army, his immediate superior; the President; the Secretary of State; Mr Churchill (through me); Mr Churchill (direct); the Foreign Secretary.'

To have so many bosses was disconcerting, to say the least of it – particularly to one who had naively taken the words Supreme Commander at their face value. Things were made worse by the fact that the two governments had conflicting policies, while individual statesmen insisted on pressing forward their own ideas in matters of detail. Typically, the wrangling over the surrender terms to be presented to the Italian government had irritated Eisenhower almost beyond endurance. To him, the issue was perfectly clear: 'The people are sick and tired of the war and want nothing but peace.' To the politi-

Far left: US troops disembarking in England ready for Eisenhower's largest operation – the invasion of Europe.

Below: Roosevelt awards Eisenhower the Legion of Merit during his trip for the Teheran Conference.

cians the piling up of clause upon clause in the surrender document was the only safeguard against the unexpected; though as Eisenhower pointed out, the unexpected 'could never be prevented by the words in a document.'

Such irritants had multiplied until, with the stalemate that set in after the capture of Naples and Foggia, his spirit was at its lowest ebb. He admitted later that had it been possible for a soldier to resign he never came nearer to throwing in his hand than in the winter of 1943. He wrote to Churchill: 'I am ready to carry out in detail any instructions that the two governments may choose to give me. All I urge is that the governments decide quickly . . . and give me a suitable directive by which my actions may be guided.' No clear directive came. The governments were continually bickering, unclear themselves as to what courses of action they should pursue. What Macmillan called 'the constant pressure of telegraphic advice on every conceivable point' was concerned mainly with criticizing Eisenhower for overasserting what

Below: The Allied invasion chiefs at a press conference in Allied Command Headquarters. Eisenhower is fourth from left.

ordered the establishment of advanced headquarters in Naples. 'Nothing elaborate,' he told Butcher, 'It does morale as much good as a hole in the head to have command living in plush hotels while the men bivouac round the mountains with the rain falling on them.' Butcher's idea of 'nothing elaborate' was Prince Umberto's hunting lodge as a personal billet for Eisenhower, with command headquarters in the Caserta Palace. Eisenhower was too harassed by the politicians to do more than lodge a token protest. 'The hell with it,' he said to Kay Summersby. 'Maybe there'll be room for all of us to kick the ball around in an office the size of Grand Central station.'

Another factor was contributing to Eisenhower's feeling of inadequacy. As a result of a deliberate leak to the press by Roosevelt – who was shrewdly testing the temperature of public response – it had come to be firmly accepted that Overlord, the greatest invasion in history, would be commanded by General George Marshall. Marshall was an obvious choice. As Chief of Staff he held the highest office in the army, with only the President, who constitutionally was commander in chief of all the armed forces, above him. His integrity and achievements went unquestioned and he had the confidence of the Allied heads of state. Eisenhower, Marshall's protégé, naturally warmed to the appointment; but what subdued his warmth was the virtual certainty that with Marshall as Supreme Commander in Europe he himself would have to swap the job for that of the Chief of Staff in Washington. His gratitude to Marshall for 'pitching

Above: Eisenhower meeting troops in England.

Right: The Allied advance in Italy.

he reasonably considered to be his authority. To these criticisms he replied with dignity that he did not see how a war could be conducted successfully if every act of the Supreme Commander had to be referred to the governments for advance approval. With an unusual edge of acerbity that was a combination of resignation and resentment he added that if he failed to carry out what was required of him he would expect to be relieved of his command, but that as long as he held that command he did not expect the authority and responsibility of his office to be diminished.

Tired of inactivity and the political backbiting, Eisenhower made several visits to the front, where continual rain hampered the operation of the air forces and small drives into the solidly established German defenses could not be exploited. He decided that headquarters at Algiers was too far away to be in proper contact with the troops and

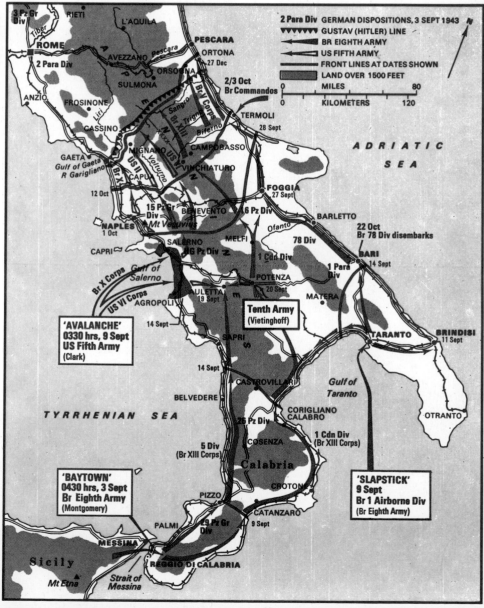

him into the fray' was enormous, but he viewed the prospect of a return to Washington without joy. He morosely told Kay, 'If I have to return to Washington, I'll be carried up to Arlington Cemetery within six months anyway.' But he evidently kept a shred of hope, for early in December he wrote to Mamie, 'What is going to happen as a result of all rumored changes in command, etc., I don't know. But no matter what does happen – I do hope I can have a visit with you before long. I know I'm a changed person – no one could go through what I've seen and not be different from what he was at the beginning. But in at least one way I'm certain of my reactions – I love you! I wish I could see you an hour to tell you how

Below: The Teheran Conference in 1943 was the first time that the three Allied leaders met to discuss strategy.

much!'

Roosevelt's object in seeking reaction to the story of Marshall's probable appointment as supreme commander of Overlord was solely political. His term as President ended in 1944 and he was anxious to judge the likelihood of his reelection. There was, as he had expected, plenty of reaction – much of it critical. The Republican element made no bones about accusing Roosevelt of chicanery in ousting Marshall so that some general with Democratic sympathies could be appointed in his place, thus ensuring the awarding of war contracts to Roosevelt's supporters. Marshall's integrity placed him above suspicion in this way, but the Republican press made it clear that no one else was. Roosevelt was satisfied. He had his reaction. He would tread warily and keep his counsel.

There were of course other candidates for the appointment. One was Alan

Brooke, another Mountbatten, who had long been invaluable in the planning of Combined Operations. It was generally accepted by the Combined Chiefs of Staff that the overall commander of Overlord would be an American because the Americans were providing by far the greater part of the men and materiel for the operation. Bedell Smith was another possibility; but he was junior in both rank and experience to Patton, Bradley and Clark, who could hardly be expected to work happily with a man who had been promoted over their heads.

While Roosevelt held his cards close to his chest, listened to advice from all quarters and said nothing, Eisenhower prepared to receive him, the other heads of state and the Combined Chiefs of Staff, for yet another conference, in Cairo. This time, the importance of Italy having been relegated to a state of nuisance value, it was to be entirely

Right: Eisenhower returns a salute at Sandhurst. His many public appearances made him well-known and well-liked.

about Overlord – or so the agenda said. However, Eisenhower did not intend that the forces commanded by Montgomery, Alexander and Clark be ignored. Questioned by the Chiefs, he told them his most important objective was the Po Valley but that he would need far more equipment – particularly landing craft – if the Po was to be reached by spring. He added ominously that if he was given the equipment it would inevitably rob Overlord, which in consequence would be delayed by three months. This pleased nobody except possibly Churchill, who still obstinately kept his mind on Turkey and the Balkans. Nevertheless, the Chiefs and statesmen were impressed by Eisenhower's clear exposition of the situation. Even Brooke, who had never warmed to Eisenhower and had doubts about his ability as a strategist, nodded in appreciation. 'If the object of the probe had been to see if Ike still had his eye on the ball,' Butcher wrote in the diary, 'he passed the test with flying colors.'

The conference moved on from Cairo to Teheran, where the results of their deliberations would be discussed with Stalin. That, anyway, was the idea but since no real decisions had been made at Cairo there seemed singularly little point. Many sessions were held, however, and at all of them there was no doubt left in the minds of the British and American representatives that Stalin was determined to have Overlord mounted in the largest possible way and even earlier than its scheduled date of 1 May 1944. It took the Combined Chiefs of Staff all their time and a great deal of acrimony to prove that an operation of such magnitude mounted before it was ready could lead only to disaster. Eventually Stalin agreed, but made it perfectly clear that he would not tolerate any delay beyond that date. He saw Churchill, with his equivocation over the Mediterranean and Balkans areas, as a potential intruder into Soviet influence in Yugoslavia. Roosevelt, Marshall and the US Secretary of War, Henry Stimson, firmly aligned themselves with Stalin in the argument. Churchill – who had a bad cold – saw no prospect of beating down such a bastion and wisely did not try.

Instead, he saw Stalin privately and told him that he had every confidence in the *idea* of Overlord but had nightmares about the possibility of the 40 or so German divisions in France being enough to throw the invaders out. 'I am not afraid about getting on shore, but about what will happen on the thirtieth, fortieth, or fiftieth day.' Stalin merely smiled an enigmatic smile which Churchill took to mean, 'It's your turn now; we've held the fort long enough.'

To conclude the Teheran Conference there was a dinner for the Russians at the British legation. It was not an easy occasion. Alan Brooke unwisely referred to the British as having suffered most during the war – hardly a diplomatic thing to say, even if true, which was in any case arguable according to what was meant by 'suffering.' Stalin then accused Brooke of being anti-Russian, whjch Brooke vehemently denied, and calm was restored only after some rather shamefaced withdrawals of offensive remarks and another round of toasts. It was during the drinking of these that Stalin turned to Churchill, on whose

left he was sitting, and asked directly 'Who will command Overlord?' Churchill could only say that so far as he knew it would be George Marshall, but that the President had not yet made up his mind. Stalin shrugged. Clearly he was indifferent; he was concerned only that Overlord should go ahead, and as soon as possible. But he could not believe that anything would come of it until a commander was appointed – 'So it must come quick, this man to command all, his name' – or, as he saw it, there would be no Overlord.

The conference now renewed itself in Cairo with Roosevelt extremely thoughtful about the most important appointment to be made so far. His main worry was that if Marshall was appointed Supreme Commander in the European theater he would in effect have to suffer a demotion, for both the United States Chief of Staff and the Combined Chiefs of Staff had superior authority over the theater commander – as Eisenhower was only too bitterly aware. Also, the Chief of Staff in Washington had to cope with the Secretary of War and Congress –

jobs for which Eisenhower was not particularly well suited. If the job of supreme chief had to go to an American – and on that point at least there was agreement – there was no alternative to Eisenhower. Roosevelt tried to inveigle Marshall into making the decision for him; but characteristically the stony-faced Chief of Staff replied that he could not judge a case that involved himself.

That was on 4 December 1943. Two days later Roosevelt, who was spending his last day in Cairo driving out to the

pyramids with Churchill, asked the Prime Minister what his views would be if he appointed Eisenhower to Overlord instead of Marshall. 'I nodded approval,' Churchill says. 'Good,' Roosevelt replied. There was a pause, then he added, 'I told Marshall I felt that I could not sleep at night with him out of the country.'

On 7 December he flew to Tunis, where he was met by Eisenhower. After the usual performance of getting the polio-stricken President into the car

they drove off together. After a few minutes of desultory conversation Roosevelt turned to Eisenhower and said, 'Well, Ike, you are going to command Overlord.'

No commander of Overlord could have said that the preparations for his command had been niggardly. Since Pfc Milburn Henke landed on 26 January 1942 the number of American soldiers in Britain had grown to 1,500,000. To the English tongue with its many dialects they had added as many more. The accents of Boston, the Bronx, the Deep South and the West mixed with those of Devon, Cumbria, Scotland and Wales.

Below: Churchill and Taylor, Eisenhower, Pratt and a naval officer visit training installations.

Right: Eisenhower talks to troops in May 1944, before the D-Day landings. Montgomery is behind him.

The Yanks were not backward in telling the host country that they were self-sufficient: Had not their commissariat said that they had brought 16,000,000 tons of everything from locomotives to dental fillings?

In the skies above the countryside with its camouflaged factories and mountains of stores 12,000 aircraft of the United States Army Air Force from time to time droned or hurtled through cloud and sunshine on errands of death and defense. Tiny ports round the coast

Left: A DUWK is loaded aboard an American LST at Portland Harbour in southern England in preparation for D-Day.

of Britain which had held nothing larger than a fishing smack for centuries had offered haven to strange craft with flat bottoms and doors in their bows from which, the local inhabitants said, tanks would crawl forth on to the land of German-held Europe. In the dockyards scarred by enemy bombing ships were quickly built and launched. Country lanes from Inverness to Devon held caches of ammunition guarded by soldiers said to be unfit for active service overseas but looking remarkably alert when suspect visitors approached their posts – indeed one of them was said to have prodded a visiting Major General in the belly and threatened to transfix him to the wall if he did not produce his identity card. The visiting officer, on a testing mission, had the lad promoted Lance Corporal with effect from that day.

The colorful uniforms of the French, the Poles, the Dutch and the Czechs invaded the blacked-out hostelries of English villages as if they were characters adrift from a production of *White Horse Inn*. Scientists in secret hideouts turned their minds and virtually unlimited funds to enterprises as far apart as the breaking of enemy codes and the uses of nuclear fission. The hills and valleys were choked with tanks on maneuvers, trains transporting enormous guns rumbled through the night. The little island, Britain, groaned under the weight of the machines of war. Eisenhower was reported as saying 'Only the great number of barrage balloons floating constantly in British skies kept the islands from sinking under the waves' – a witty comment that was more likely to have been invented by Harry Butcher.

The Supreme Commander arrived in London from North Africa on 14 January 1944 and was welcomed with a tremendous reception at the Dorchester, Park Lane, where he was given a suite which is still called The Eisenhower Suite. Montgomery, Bradley, Patton and Spaatz came with him. 'Jumbo takes over in Med' the newspapers reassuringly announced for the benefit of readers who might have supposed North Africa and Italy to have been forgotten – 'Jumbo' being Field Marshal Sir Henry Maitland Wilson, a man of unusual girth and

height who had succeeded Eisenhower as Supreme Commander in the Mediterranean Theater. The press, limited in size because of paper restrictions and carefully watched by the Ministry of Information, overlooked nothing that could extend the field of speculation regarding the Second Front. Inferences were draw from trivialities and were blown up to dramatic size. When Montgomery was spotted buying a book in a Piccadilly bookshop great play was made with the fact that the book was a novel, *Anthony Adverse*, by an American author, Hervey Allen, and that it was set in the time of the Napoleonic wars. There were murmurings of 'Significant, surely?' though no one could precisely pinpoint the significance. But it made good copy and harmless gossip, though everyone was being reminded in advertisements and on the radio that 'Careless Talk Costs Lives.'

Rumor mongering with a seemingly dangerous potential was smartly dealt with. Hearing of a breach of secrecy by a USAAF officer, Eisenhower immediately reduced him in rank from Major General to Colonel and sent him back to America. Careless talk of a different kind brought Patton into disrepute when he arrogantly said in public that after the war Britain and the U.S. would rule the world. 'I wish to God he'd watch his words,' Eisenhower said, and gave him a dressing-down. He was too good a soldier to be sent home.

Another man who had to watch his words was schoolmaster Mr L S Dawe, in the department of English at St Paul's School, Hammersmith (later to be Montgomery's headquarters), who was one of the compilers of the *Daily Telegraph*'s crossword puzzle. He'd used the words MULBERRY and OVERLORD in two successive puzzles, and as these happened to be code names connected with the invasion there was an immediate investigation by Intelligence officers. They found that the choice of the words was purely coincidental; but poor Mr Dawe had a wearing time proving it. Also given a grilling was an unfortunate trainee teletype operator at the Associated Press Bureau who had failed to grasp the fact that before practicing transmissions it was well to ensure that the key completing the circuit was not pressed down. She concocted a message announcing that invasions had

Left: Troops training in England. D-Day preparations were enormous – Eisenhower had 3,000,000 men under his command.

begun in France, and Eisenhower's headquarters had to issue a speedy denial before it actually got into the press.

Such worries, though, were small compared with those Eisenhower had to cope with on the strategical front – particularly in the air arm. Tedder, who was his immediate deputy in the chain of command; Portal, Chief of the Air Staff; Harris of Bomber Command; and Leigh-Mallory, Commander in Chief of the Allied Expeditionary Air Force, all had different notions on the part the air arm was to play in Overlord. There were also intense conflicts of character between them. 'Bomber' Harris was immoveable in his belief in 'area' bombing to disrupt industry and terrorize the civilian population, and his 'thousand bomber' raids had had a limited success, though at immense cost in lives and planes and reaping considerable moral reproach from those who saw the razing of such cities as Cologne as senseless. Leigh-Mallory, whom Harris disliked intensely, was head of Fighter Command and an advocate of what became known as the Transportation Plan, which concentrated on enemy communications and supplies, and which in the event proved to be entirely successful in hampering the resistance of Hitler's forces in Normandy

Left: GIs armed with Garand rifles and Bazookas march down to their landing craft at Tor Bay, Devon, England.

when the bridgehead was established. Portal had been Harris's predecessor at Bomber Command and had shared his views on area bombing. Being less pigheaded, however, he revised his ideas in the light of experience and fell in with Leigh-Mallory's views to some extent. Eisenhower told Butcher, 'These gentlemen are stiff-necked Britishers who get in each other's way and mine too; and I sometimes wish to God I could kick them all in the butt.' He was, perhaps naturally, far more at home with his own countryman Carl Spaatz. Spaatz held a compromise view: he was with Harris on the effectiveness of intensive bombing but wanted it concentrated on synthetic-oil production plants. Eisenhower half agreed with him; but he could also see the viewpoints of Leigh-Mallory and Portal and could understand their English distaste for the untidy, frequently unshaven, crumple-faced American. 'That was his trouble,' Bedell Smith recorded. 'He could understand everybody's viewpoint. Sometimes his understanding robbed him of a viewpoint of his own.' This was not always the case. Two or three times at conferences that threatened to develop into slanging matches he talked about quitting. Churchill says that the rather prissy words 'If the unhelpful British attitude continues, then I will go home' were invested with a great deal of power and meaning when 'spat out across a conference table without any of the charm of the ear-to-ear grin that normally splits Ike's face.' The muddle and wrangling was never properly sorted out. 'From an

Below: US infantry practice assault landings on a beach in Devon in May 1944.

Above: GIs march through Torquay, Devon, prior to embarking for the invasion of Normandy.

organizational point of view it was lousy,' Spaatz said, referring to the intricate air command structure. General Frederick Morgan, who had been chief of planning for Overlord, and had now handed over his plans to Supreme Headquarters, Allied Expeditionary Force, later recorded, 'It will, I think, be a considerable time before anybody will be able to set down in the form of an organizational diagram the channels through which General Eisenhower's orders reached his aircraft.'

Eisenhower had less difficulty assembling his army commanders, 'It was a cinch compared with the prima donnas of the air,' he noted. He already had Montgomery, Bradley and Patton. To them he added Major Generals Joe Collins and Leonard Gerow his old buddy, plus a West Point classmate of Patton's, Everett S Hughes. 'Jobs for the boys,' Churchill remarked; but he could not gainsay the fact that Eisenhower's selection of officers was meticulously fair in its division of British and American personnel, even though his staff grew to the enormous number of 5000 by the time Overlord was launched. Collins, whom Eisenhower had known in the Philippines, was scheduled to become a corps commander, Hughes a sort of

quidnunc who would be attached to Patton as his Chief of Staff and hold what Eisenhower called 'a watching brief.' What he was to watch was not specified; but in all walks of life, in peace and war, there are those whose undercover information is useful. Less than useful – in fact a burden – was Washington-sponsored Lieutenant General J C H Lee who had the impressive-sounding appointment of 'Deputy Theater Commander,' a job concerned mainly with getting equipment stockpiled in the right places for use at the right time. Like Montgomery, he was on good terms with God and apparently used his private line to heaven to get divine approval for a great many ostentatious activities. Even Bedell Smith resented being outranked 'by a Holy Joe with a Public Relations outfit like a film mogul.'

The term was not inept to describe the whole setup of Overlord during the preparation period: The cast of thousands, the bouts of temperament thrown by the principals, the PR men building up the publicity, the front-office administrators anxious solely for a success, the epic grandeur of the sets. There was also the inescapable feeling that all was transitory – a feeling emphasized by the scarred landscape and

Right: General Eisenhower's message of encouragement to the Allied Expeditionary Force before D-Day.

the existence of 'transit camps' through which hundreds of thousands of troops were being funnelled as they gradually made their way from locations in Scotland, Cumbria, Lancashire and Yorkshire, from the midlands and Wales, from the Dukeries and the Wash, the Home Counties and westward from the very tip of Cornwall, to embarkation points – many of them illusory to deceive the enemy – along the southern and eastern shores of Dorset, Hampshire, Sussex and Kent.

Eisenhower had several headquarters between which Kay Summersby transported him, sometimes in a bulletproof Packard, sometimes a jeep. Grosvenor Square was, in the Supreme Commander's words, 'so grand I could hear Mom quoting some text against getting above myself.' Bushy Park, out near his previous weekend cottage at Richmond, was squalid in comparison – prefabricated huts and a dreary office with flaking paint and creaking floors in which he had a desk round which from time to time would crowd the navy, army and air commanders, the Prime Minister and the Chiefs of Staff – and once or twice, the King. Then there was St Paul's School, in Hammersmith, where Montgomery had been educated and where he set up the HQ of 21st Army Group, which combined the United States First Army under Omar Bradley and the British Second Army

SUPREME HEADQUARTERS
ALLIED EXPEDITIONARY FORCE

Soldiers, Sailors and Airmen of the Allied Expeditionary Force!

You are about to embark upon the Great Crusade, toward which we have striven these many months. The eyes of the world are upon you. The hopes and prayers of liberty-loving people everywhere march with you. In company with our brave Allies and brothers-in-arms on other Fronts, you will bring about the destruction of the German war machine, the elimination of Nazi tyranny over the oppressed peoples of Europe, and security for ourselves in a free world.

Your task will not be an easy one. Your enemy is well trained, well equipped and battle-hardened. He will fight savagely.

But this is the year 1944 ! Much has happened since the Nazi triumphs of 1940-41. The United Nations have inflicted upon the Germans great defeats, in open battle, man-to-man. Our air offensive has seriously reduced their strength in the air and their capacity to wage war on the ground. Our Home Fronts have given us an overwhelming superiority in weapons and munitions of war, and placed at our disposal great reserves of trained fighting men. The tide has turned ! The free men of the world are marching together to Victory !

I have full confidence in your courage, devotion to duty and skill in battle. We will accept nothing less than full Victory !

Good Luck ! And let us all beseech the blessing of Almighty God upon this great and noble undertaking.

Dwight D Eisenhower

Above: Hundreds of barrage balloons were used to protect the enormous forces gathered for the invasion.

under General Sir Miles Dempsey. There were also of course the individual arm commanders' headquarters – Leigh-Mallory's at Stanmore in Middlesex, Tedder's at Southwick in Hampshire, Admiral Sir Bertram Ramsay's at Portsmouth – 'which I'm everlastingly shuttling between like a messenger boy, holding conferences which plan and plan and plan. . . .'

The basic plan for the invasion had been worked out during many months prior to Eisenhower's arrival in London from the Mediterranean Theater by General Morgan. Morgan had seen the initial assault as being by three divisions transported by landing craft and two airborne divisions. Their object would be to establish a bridgehead on a 25-mile front from the Orne to the Vire. Eisenhower saw both the breadth of the attack and the size of the assault force as too limited. He continually referred back to Churchill's outline of Roundup: 'Landings or feints should be planned . . . first object to get ashore in large numbers . . . seizure of at least four important ports must be accomplished . . . unless we are prepared to commit the immense

forces. . . .' He doubled the breadth of the front until it stretched for 50 miles, from Cabourg to Quinéville. Then he reinforced the assault forces with another two seaborne divisions and one more airborne division. There were objections from Morgan, who was offended because he had planned for minimum losses rather than maximum gains and thought Mont-

gomery, 'an upstart from Italy,' had unduly influenced Eisenhower. In fact nobody had influenced Eisenhower, who in his smooth way listened to everybody and shrewdly added to and subtracted from their thoughts and suggestions until there was a mixture of elements that appealed to him. On those elements he based his own designs. It amused him to see and hear comments about his lack of boldness: 'Generally speaking the British press tries to show that my contributions in the Mediterranean were administrative accomplishments and friendliness in welding an Allied team. They dislike to believe that I had anything particularly to do with campaigns. They don't use the words initiative and boldness in talking of me – but often do in speaking of Alex and Monty.' The press could not altogether be blamed. The flamboyant and the sensational were always easier for them to present than the activities – in any case 90 percent secret – of the mastermind. 'One Patton or Montgomery is worth four Eisenhowers,' one editor told his staff.

Lee also had huge publicity value, just as a bit-part player can sometimes outshine the star. He was frequently to be seen escorting Lady Mountbatten, wife of Lord Louis, Chief of Com-

Below: Eisenhower talks to a member of an Airborne Engineer Unit constructing an air strip.

Right: US airborne forces check their equipment before boarding their Horsa gliders on 5 June 1944.

bined Operations, to theaters and social occasions. A catchphrase of Monty's was as potent as one of Churchill's. When he urged his troops to pray that 'The Lord mighty in battle' should be on their side he had half the population flipping through the Book of Psalms in search of other gems. When it leaked out that Monty had irritably countered a proposed visit by the Prime Minister to Portsmouth with the declaration, 'If Winnie comes down here he'll not only be a great bore but also may well attract undue attention. Why in hell doesn't he go and smoke his cigar in Dover Castle and be seen with the Lord Mayor? It would fix the Germans' attentions on Calais,' the leak had to be stopped with an admonitory official finger.

The enemy of course knew perfectly well that an invasion was planned. It would have been impossible to keep the immense buildup of men and arms from them. They had access to the same information about weather and tides as had the Allies. Their agents had labored for months, indeed years, to amass the scraps of information that were fed back to the Abwehr; and the corresponding British Secret Service had labored equally to see that as much as possible of the information thus garnered was misleading. The main ploy was to persuade Hitler to think that the real invasion would be launched in the area Dunkirk-Boulogne and that the Normandy landing was only a feint. It was the Sicily trick all over again. Hitler conveniently swallowed the misinformation hook, line and sinker despite the warnings of his navy chiefs that Cherbourg and Le Havre had been left virtually undamaged by Allied air raids and therefore might be assumed to be important to the invasion effort. Obstinately, for he had never been a naval man, he discounted their observations and accepted the army's view that the strongest defense should be concentrated in the Pas de Calais area. It was duly concentrated. He did not – could not – know when D-Day would be. Eisenhower himself did not know. A May date had been promised to Stalin, but even before Eisenhower had decided on three more divisions than Morgan had planned it was clear that a big

enough assault force would not be ready before June, possibly later. Weather, light and tides were the prime considerations. Tides would be right in the first week in June if cloud, wind and rain did not combine to obscure the moonlight necessary for airborne landings or roughen the sea enough to hamper the beach landings. Similar tidal conditions would not prevail until two weeks later. So if, as was necessary, everything was made ready by 1 June and the enterprise was then delayed there would be not only a greater chance of the enemy penetrating the carapace of secrecy but also of Allied morale being stretched to breaking point in a battle of nervous tension. Eisenhower opted for early June – 'The first suitable day will be the 5th,' he noted. 'And that will be it.'

All was ready by 1 June. To transport and protect the 200,000 men of the invasion force there were 5000 ships of one sort and another; backing them up was a Tactical Air Force of 6000 Allied aircraft; and ready to reinforce and push out once the bridgehead was established were another 40 divisions on standby call. But on 3 June there was ominous news from the department upon which so much depended – the meteorological office. In the person of its principal, Group Captain Stagg, the meteorologists of the office with one Cassandran voice declared that they could see nothing for 5 June but 'a cloud base too low for flying plus stormy wind, followed by at least twenty-four hours of weather so unsettled that they would not venture to forecast.'

Nevertheless on 4 June they found what literally was a break in the clouds. 'I have no good news,' said Stagg; 'but I have encouraging news: a new weather front will move up the Channel in the wake of the stormy stuff tomorrow. The rain will stop tomorrow night, the wind fall, and the clouds rise enough for aircraft to operate soon after midnight.' But he left an escape route for his office: 'They've done their best; but they can't guarantee even those tolerable conditions.'

Earlier that day Eisenhower had received a teletype that General Mark Clark's victorious Fifth Army had

Right: Eisenhower gives the Order of the Day, 'Full Victory – Nothing Else,' to paratroopers about to board their aircraft.

Below: Part of the massive invasion force assembled for D-Day lying off the English South Coast.

Above: US troops aboard an LCI. Some
57,500 US troops landed on Omaha and
Utah beaches on the first day.

entered Rome. It had been an arduous year-long campaign in Italy and it had not succeeded in drawing off forces from the Eastern Front; but it had kept tied down some German troops who might have been switched to Normandy if Hitler had rightly judged the scene of the invasion. Eisenhower knew nothing of them, and if he had would have been too concerned with his immediate problem to bother. He asked Butcher to wire congratulations to Clark, canvassed the opinions of Leigh-Mallory and Tedder, of Bedell Smith and Montgomery, on D-Day being 6 June, and sent out the order cancelling the extant launch date of the 5th. The Air Chiefs were hesitant about committing their

forces for the 6th, even with Stagg's mild encouragement; Bedell Smith and Monty were ready to risk it. For one with so onerous a decision resting on his shoulders Eisenhower seemed to his colleagues 'quite calm apart from his nervous chain-smoking,' as the austere, nonsmoking, teetotal Montgomery noted with distaste. At 21.45 hours on Sunday 4 June 1944 the Supreme Commander gave his decision for the 6th: 'Okay. Let's go.'

Having committed the vast forces under his command to the biggest invasion in history Eisenhower left Admiral Ramsay's headquarters and returned to the trailer caravan that was his forward headquarters. There, with Kay Summersby brewing him coffee, he

prepared a communiqué that he prayed would never have to be sent but was in a sense an insurance against the possibility of failure:

'Our landings in the Cherbourg-Havre area have failed to gain a satisfactory foothold and I have withdrawn the troops. My decision to attack at this time and place was based upon the best information available. The troops, the air and the Navy did all that Bravery and devotion to duty could do. If any blame or fault attaches to the attempt it is mine alone.'

Then he poured coffee, lay back in his armchair and relaxed with a Western that had that day arrived from Mamie. It was called *Six-shooter Trail*.

Below: USS *Nevada* and USS *Texas* in line astern prior to D-Day.

7: VICTORY

The basic assault plan was to establish five separate bridgeheads on beaches the names of which have become as familiar as those of Verdun and Passchendaele: Utah and Omaha to the west; Gold, Juno, and Sword to the east. Bradley's First US Army was assigned to Utah and Omaha, Dempsey's Second (British and Canadian) Army to Gold, Juno, and Sword. The objective was a 10-mile thrust into Normandy by the end of the first day, including, most importantly, the capture of the port of Caen.

The plan went awry. Too much caution on the part of the commanders plus serious jamming on the beaches from Ouistreham to Arromanches, which prevented rapid progress inland, held things up till afternoon. By that time Von Rundstedt, in charge of the German opposition, had ordered forward a panzer division which checked the Allied advance. The historian AJP Taylor says sternly, 'The dalliance on the beach was Gallipoli all over again.'

There were other setbacks. At Omaha beach Leonard Gerow's V Corps met stiff opposition, the effect of which was increased by landings having been misjudged and made too far offshore so that many landing craft and tanks were swamped and sank. The tanks that got ashore had not been fitted with flails and many were blown up on mines. Engineers sent in to clear the beach suffered terrible casualties, and hundreds of assault troops were put out of action by violent seasickness. Heavy crossfire caused many more casualties, and it was not until nightfall that the assault could be restarted. This time the landings were successful and held Omaha throughout the night while further reinforcements were brought in nearer the shore; but over 3000 men were lost, together with 50 tanks, 26 guns, and 60 landing craft.

Eisenhower crossed the Channel next morning and amid the turmoil on Omaha beach conferred with Bradley. The plan was changed. Instead of driving inland, the forces on Utah and Omaha were to attempt to link up with each other at Carentan and form a continuous front before pushing inland. He also saw Montgomery, who said the battle was going well – which in a sense it was. None of the D-Day objectives was achieved – it was a month before Caen fell – but the five separate bridgeheads had linked up within three days and by 12 June the invasion forces had pushed 15 miles inland on a front of 60 miles. 'But the losses are not light,' Eisenhower recorded. On 6 June alone there had

Left: Troops gather round for Eisenhower's autograph on his visit to France on 26 July 1944.

Below: Troops in an LCVP (Landing Craft, Vehicle Personnel) head toward Omaha beach on 6 June 1944.

Left: Allied leaders confer in France: from left, Crerar, Montgomery, Stimpson and Cunningham.

Below left: The Mulberry artificial harbor at Arromanches provided a much-needed sheltered anchorage.

been 9000 casualties. It was not quite the same to see the figures mount as to regard Churchill's dispassionate observation in the Roundup design, 'The phase of sudden violence, irrespective of losses, being over, the further course of the campaign may follow the normal and conventional lines. . . .' '"Irrespective of losses" is a cruel Phrase,' Eisenhower said in one of his hasty letters to Mamie; 'but unfortunately it is a practical one.'

The campaign did not in every respect follow the 'normal and conventional lines.' For one thing, the weather took a hand. On 19 June a great storm struck the French coast and one of the famous 'Mulberry' prefabricated harbors was ripped apart while it was being unloaded. This was the very day on which the invasion would have been launched had Eisenhower not taken the chance on the 6th. He sent a message to Stagg: 'Thanks, and thank the gods of war we went when

Below: Marines wade ashore at Sword beach with their equipment, including Welbikes.

Above: A victim of the first assault wave,
an American soldier lies dead beside a
beach obstacle.

Below: LSTs (Landing Ship Tank) landing
vital supplies after the initial assault on
Omaha Beach.

Above: A US Navy expert disassembles a German remote controlled miniature tank on Omaha Beach.

Above left: Gliders and tow planes of the Ninth Air Force. Paratroopers were dropped in the rear of enemy lines

Above: The headlines of *The Philadelphia Inquirer* announce the invasion of Europe.

them he was not prepared to interfere with the tactical decisions of the man on the spot.

There followed a situation reminiscent of Italy – stalemate. Runstedt and Rommel met Hitler near Rheims on 17 June and planned a counterattack towards Bayeaux with a Panzer corps Hitler had recalled from the Eastern front; but the launching of it took too long and Montgomery smashed it before it achieved any force. But in general there was very little movement. Bradley took Cherbourg on 27 June and tried to break out of the Cotentin; but the hedgerow country was easily defended and progress was slow. After visiting the front from 1–4 July Eisenhower returned to London and reported to Marshall, 'The going is extremely tough.' It might, he thought, be easier on Montgomery's front. He was disabused of that notion by Tedder – not about the ease of going but about Montgomery's caution, which, Tedder said, was excessive and involved far too much preparation and too little energy of the 'pushing' type. Also, Montgomery was blaming the air forces for a static

Below: German prisoners of war carry a wounded comrade to an Allied landing craft for medical treatment.

we did.'

Also, the plan was to some extent altered by Montgomery, who was something of a law unto himself. Finding himself unable to capture Caen he told the CIGS that his plan was 'to pull the enemy on to Second Army so as to make it easier for First Army to expand and extend the quicker.' Since this meant subordinating his own achievements to those of the Americans it seemed out of character, to say the least of it. Nor was it the battle Eisenhower wanted fought. But it must be admitted that Eisenhower did not – as he could have done – countermand the order and tell Montgomery to get on with capturing Caen and not make a siege of it. Challenged about it after the war he said that he was a clear supporter of the American army tradition that gave commanders independence, and although he was prepared to lay down policy decisions and stick to

Above: Access to the beaches after D-Day was controlled and regulated by beachmasters.

situation which was rapidly deteriorating into one of trench warfare. Eisenhower was furious but saw that he must handle Montgomery tactfully. He wrote to him saying, 'We must use all possible energy in a determined effort to prevent a stalemate or of facing the necessity of fighting a major defensive battle with the slight depth we now have in the bridge-head.' There was no appreciable response, which was not really surprising since Eisenhower in attempting tact had achieved only flabbiness. It was surely a moment when tradition should have been thrown to the winds and a firm order given. Instead, Eisenhower complained to Churchill and asked the Prime Minister to 'persuade Monty to get on his bicycle and start moving.' This caused a blazing row between Churchill and Brooke. Churchill was not a great admirer of Montgomery and thought Eisenhower was right to urge him forward. Brooke took this as abuse of Montgomery and asked Churchill 'if he could not trust his Generals for five minutes without belittling them.' Eisenhower, ever a thorn in Brooke's side, was made the scapegoat for resembling 'a sneaky schoolboy going to the head-master.'

Caen was eventually taken, but with little praise for Montgomery, who was considered by American newsmen and commentators to have reverted to the trench tactics of the First World War. Eisenhower was headlined as having been 'mad' that 7000 tons of bombs had been expended on an advance of seven miles. There was talk of raising Montgomery to the peerage and making him Governor of Malta, 'or something similarly harmless,' as Tedder put it. But Churchill had to move warily. Montgomery had been built up as a star, the hero of El Alamein, and had enormous prestige in the public eye. As a statesman Churchill was inevitably concerned about political reactions if Montgomery was sacked.

A distraction arrived in the form of an attempt on Hitler's life by conspirators who believed he was leading Germany to defeat. The attempt was ham-fisted and the circumstances unpropitious. The bomb that was planted in Hitler's conference room at Rastenburg on 20 July 1944 split the Führer's trousers, bruised his buttocks and singed his hair; otherwise he was uninjured. The conspirators were caught and hanged with nooses of piano wire after a 'trial' before the People's Court. Hitler later revelled in the film made of the hanging. Then the war went on, unimpeded by a mild sensation with which the Allied press made great play.

Less pleasant distractions in the form of Hitler's 'secret weapons,' the V-1 'buzzbomb' and the V-2 rocket, hit battle-scarred London and its environs in June and continued until the end of the year, by which time their launching sites had been destroyed by the advancing Allied armies and the indefatigable efforts of the bomber squadrons. The capital 'took it' for what was to prove the last time.

Eisenhower, showing himself from time to time in London and being acknowledged by the American press 'as the greatest thing since icecream,' had his own troubles, not least of which were the continuing quarrels among the Generals. In many ways they were immature, like children, shouting at each other if an advantage was stolen. Characteristically, Patton, whose Third US Army had arrived in Normandy,

Below: The Supreme Commander watches the landings from the deck of a warship on 7 June 1944.

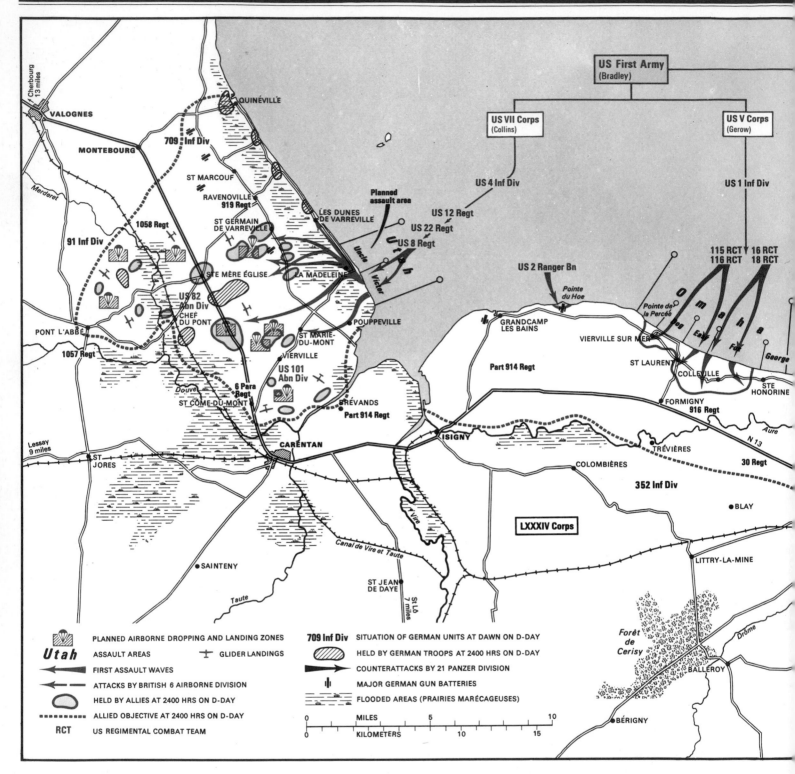

Utah — PLANNED AIRBORNE DROPPING AND LANDING ZONES

Utah ASSAULT AREAS — GLIDER LANDINGS

FIRST ASSAULT WAVES

ATTACKS BY BRITISH 6 AIRBORNE DIVISION

HELD BY ALLIES AT 2400 HRS ON D-DAY

ALLIED OBJECTIVE AT 2400 HRS ON D-DAY

RCT US REGIMENTAL COMBAT TEAM

709 Inf Div SITUATION OF GERMAN UNITS AT DAWN ON D-DAY

HELD BY GERMAN TROOPS AT 2400 HRS ON D-DAY

COUNTERATTACKS BY 21 PANZER DIVISION

MAJOR GERMAN GUN BATTERIES

FLOODED AREAS (PRAIRIES MARÉCAGEUSES)

MILES 0 5 10

KILOMETERS 0 10 15

wanted his share of the limelight. Patton said Bradley was 'a man of great mediocrity'; Bradley referred to Montgomery as 'third rate'; Montgomery told Brooke (who attempted to implement the request) that he should 'remove Ike's hand from control of the land battle'; and Eisenhower himself said again in another moment of stress, 'If the unhelpful British attitude continues, then I will go home' – the remark of a petulant child at a party.

Of course the makers of these remarks considered they had good reasons for making them. In their memoirs they guard them with the justifying circumstances or refer to biographers as having isolated them from contextual events and therefore left a misleading impression. But the impression was not misleading to Eisenhower. He was conscious that Patton, forcefully pushing his Third Army out of the bridgehead on 25 July in a darting operation appropriately named Cobra, 'bellyaching like all-out because Monty's got the gas and he hasn't and needs it more' was fully justified. Regardless, Patton dug his toes in for a long hard battle with the enemy, gained the limelight with his flamboyant tactics and continued to spit out contemptuous remarks about Montgomery, with whose 21st Army Group he wanted to link up across a wide gap flanking the town of Falaise, thereby cutting off the bulk of the German

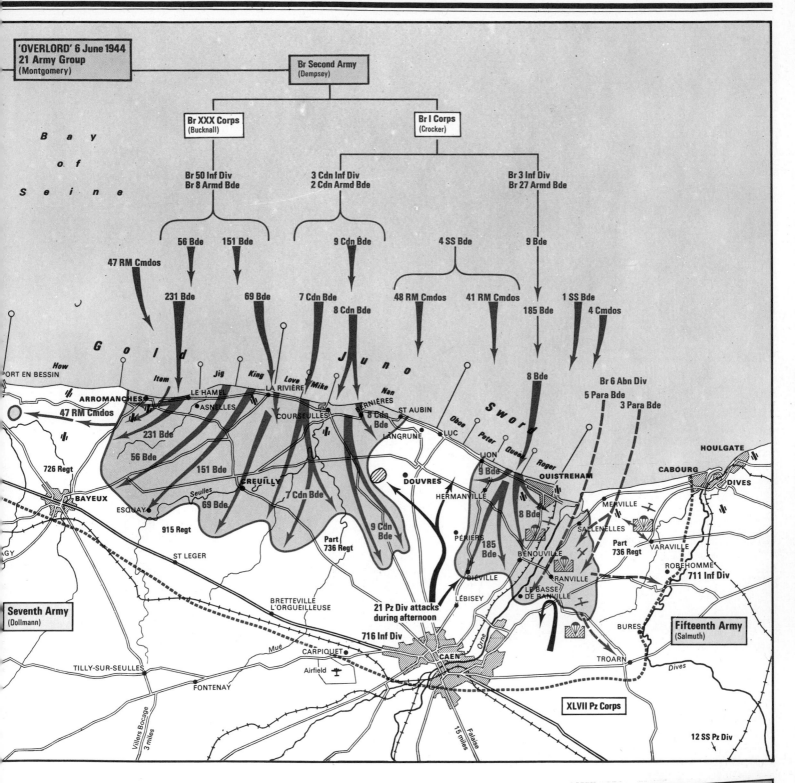

'OVERLORD' 6 June 1944
21 Army Group
(Montgomery)

Br Second Army
(Dempsey)

Br XXX Corps
(Bucknall)

Br I Corps
(Crocker)

Br 50 Inf Div
Br 8 Armd Bde

3 Cdn Inf Div
2 Cdn Armd Bde

Br 3 Inf Div
Br 27 Armd Bde

Above: Map of the D-Day landings.

Right: The *Daily Herald*'s headlines on 7 June.

army. Montgomery was too cautious for Patton's taste and he fumed at Eisenhower to be allowed to go on to Falaise 'and drive the British into the sea for another Dunkirk' – a remark hardly in the best interests of Anglo-American relations and fully justifying Eisenhower's reproachful 'George, you talk

Far left: Eisenhower under the B-26 which Arnold gave him to visit the front line in France.

Left: Britain was attacked by the deadly V-1 bomb until the invasion forces overran the launching sites.

Below left: The hedgerows of the Normandy countryside provided excellent defensive cover and delayed the advance.

Below: Eisenhower with the King on an inspection of the battlefront in France.

Eisenhower took over command of the combined land forces from Montgomery. This was a significant moment in British history. Great Britain, hitherto an equal of the United States, dwindled into a satellite: by the end of the war there were three times as many American as British troops in Europe.'

The invasion of the south of France, originally codenamed Anvil, had been planned the previous year as a sort of preliminary to Overlord. It had caused great argument. Churchill had opposed it for purely selfish reasons: it would have meant taking troops from Italy, from the campaign that he had hoped would give entry to Germany through the back door of the Balkans. When it eventually assumed some kind of life in August 1944 it was, as Mr Taylor says, too much.'

However, thanks largely to Patton's typically aggressive tactics, the battle of Normandy was won by mid-August and the Germans who escaped from the Falaise pocket fell back to the Seine. Field Marshal Von Kluge, who had succeeded Rundstedt as commander of Army Group B and, like Rommel, was suspected of complicity in the bomb plot against Hitler, urged the Führer to surrender after the Falaise defeat and was summarily dismissed on 17 August. He committed suicide and was replaced by Field Marshal Model.

As historian AJP Taylor so truly says, 'There was now no halting place for the Germans in France. Their shattered forces streamed back toward the German frontier. The Allied advance seemed to have become a victory march. On 15 August . . . some 50,000 American troops landed in the south of France. They encountered little resistance and advanced almost unimpeded up the valley of the Rhône. Militarily the landing in the south of France had little significance. The German forces there would have had to withdraw in any case once the north was lost. . . . During the rest of August the Allied armies rolled forward, liberating most of France and Belgium. They took things easy . . . a "war is won" attitude of mind prevailed in all ranks. There were now over two million Allied troops in France – three-fifths of them American. On 1 September

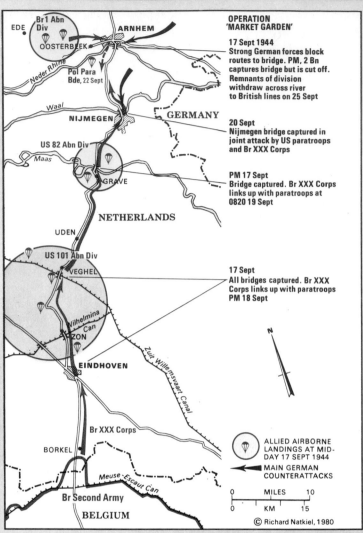

OPERATION 'MARKET GARDEN'

17 Sept 1944
Strong German forces block routes to bridge. PM, 2 Bn captures bridge but is cut off. Remnants of division withdraw across river to British lines on 25 Sept

20 Sept
Nijmegen bridge captured in joint attack by US paratroops and Br XXX Corps

PM 17 Sept
Bridge captured. Br XXX Corps links up with paratroops at 0820 19 Sept

17 Sept
All bridges captured. Br XXX Corps links up with paratroops PM 18 Sept

ⓒ Allied airborne landings at mid-day 17 Sept 1944

← Main German counterattacks

© Richard Natkiel, 1980

Above: Bradley, Weyland and Patton confer at Patton's HQ in France.

Above right: Operation Market Garden, Montgomery's ill-fated attack.

Below: Eisenhower thought the threat of a landing in Southern France might help Overlord more than an actual landing.

superfluous. But it remained a controversial issue, debated by historians long after the war ended.

Another cause of controversy was Eisenhower's strategy for the continuation of the advance to the Rhine and into Germany, which was planned well before he assumed total command of the combined land forces on 1 September and brought his advanced headquarters forward to Granville, some 400 miles from the battlefront. But the immediate cause of another outbreak of petulance among the generals was Eisenhower's praise of Montgomery at a press conference he called on 31 August to announce that 'as previously planned' (which it was) he was taking over total command of the land forces next day. The press had been extremely critical of what they had seen as 'slow progress' on Montgomery's part after D-Day – particularly the delay in the capture of Caen – and would no doubt interpret Eisenhower's total command as demotion for Montgomery. Such a view must be corrected before it gained any ground.

'So,' Eisenhower said, 'the time has come when we have broken out of the initial beachhead, and General Bradley is taking over his part of the job, reporting directly to S.H.A.E.F. headquarters, and anyone that interprets this as a demotion for General Montgomery

simply won't look facts in the face. He is not only my very close and warm friend, but a man with whom I have worked for two years, and for whom I have a tremendous admiration, one of the great soldiers of this or any other war. I will not tolerate the slightest criticism of his so-called "slow" progress at Caen after D-Day. Every foot of the ground the enemy lost at Caen was like losing ten miles anywhere else. Every piece of dust there was more than a diamond to him.'

Eisenhower's praise and emphasis on their friendly relationship notwithstanding, Montgomery continued to be a thorn in Eisenhower's side during the early days of September. Although he knew that the Supreme Commander's taking over of the ground battle was a scheduled event, Montgomery resented it deeply. He was never a man who could bear to hand over control; and with some justification he felt himself to be a better General in action than Eisenhower because he had far greater experience. He brooded and showed his resentment by refusing to go to Eisenhower's headquarters at Granville to discuss plans, offering feeble excuses that made it necessary for Eisenhower to go to him. Eisenhower knew perfectly well what Montgomery was resentful about: he wanted to steal the glory from Patton's

Third Army and make the winning thrust to Berlin and the final triumph. As Eisenhower rightly saw it, any such achievement would be tantamount to telling Marshall and the American people that their army and the huge amount of equipment they had raised was to be used only as a 'backing up' force. Such a move would be impossible; but, sensitive as always to other people's foibles, he played along with Montgomery, even at some painful inconvenience, for he had wrenched his knee in a slight airplane accident and was walking with a stick.

On 10 September Eisenhower and Montgomery met aboard Eisenhower's plane. Staff officers and even Kay Summersby had been excluded – again in deference to Montgomery, who always demanded the exclusive ear of the Supreme Commander when he wanted to give him a dressing down. This time he went too far in his criticism of Eisenhower's methods and earned a mild reproach:

'You can't talk to me like that, Monty. I'm your boss.'

Montgomery apologized for his insubordination, paused, and then laid before Eisenhower his plan for a 'short cut' to Berlin. It would involve cooperation rather than rivalry between British and American forces and would get all the Allied armies into the north German

Left: British vehicles crossing the Nijmegen Bridge after its capture on 21 9 1944.

plains before winter. 'From there,' Teddar recalled after the war, 'according to Monty everything would be a piece of cake.'

Supplies were the crux of the matter; and although 'Holy Joe' Lee, divested of the publicity apparatus that had limelighted him in England, was proving extremely efficient in seeing that supplies were where they were supposed to be when they were wanted, he could only 'Praise the Lord and pass the ammunition' when it was available. The demands of the Allied forces were astronomically vast; the output of American and British factories was also vast; but air raids, shipping losses and expenditure in battle were all limiting factors. Eisenhower as Supreme Commander had to decide which part of his army had to have priority, bearing in mind the availability of road and rail transport. And he had decided that Bradley and Patton were to make the thrust.

Montgomery's bold and imaginative plan had the advantage over Bradley's more conventional idea – of an offensive across the Rhine and into Germany with properly planned artillery support and supplies established at the railheads – in that it would 'catch the Hun on the run before he has time to organize defenses.' Its great disadvantage, of course, was that its demands on supplies would be enormous and would necessarily involve a reversal of Eisenhower's decision to give priority to Bradley. The essence of the plan was to cross into Germany over the Dutch rivers Maas and Waal by capturing bridges at Nijmegen, Eindhoven and Arnhem. The bridges would be secured by paratroops of the US 82nd

and 101st Airborne Divisions (Eindhoven and Nijmegen), and the British 1st Airborne Division (Arnhem). That achieved, the British XXX Corps would surge forward before the Germans had time to bring up reinforcements for a counterattack. Eisenhower's first thoughts were that the plan was crazy.

Bradley simply could not understand how Montgomery ever conceived it. He was to write in his memoirs, 'Had the pious teetotaling Montgomery wobbled into H.Q. with a hangover I could not have been more astonished than I was by the daring venture he proposed. For in contrast to the conservative tactics Montgomery ordinarily chose, the Arnhem attack was to be made over a 60-mile carpet of airborne troops.' But the more Eisenhower thought about it the more he thought it worth the risk. Bradley's forces had met stiffening German resistance to their progress after crossing the Moselle and had scarcely moved forward in two weeks. Despite the objections raised by the American

Right: The airborne landings at Arnhem. At first, Eisenhower thought that this operation was too risky.

Left: General Marshall was considered as commander of American forces in Europe, but was too useful in Washington.

Generals, Eisenhower decided that Montgomery should have extra supplies to enable him to launch Operation Market-Garden – which, if it was successful, would aid the recovery of the port of Antwerp. With Antwerp fully operational and in Allied hands there would be considerable shortening of the supply lines and an easy positioning of 21st Army Group for a broad-fronted drive into Germany.

Market-Garden began well. The American airborne troops caught the Germans by surprise and captured their bridges; the British paratroopers also managed to capture and hold the north end of the Arnhem bridge. But after that difficulties developed rapidly. Once again the weather took a hand and the German defenses proved to be far more flexible than had been bargained for. It was impossible to get reinforcements to the British paratroopers who were cut off at the north end of the Arnhem bridge, and after a gallant stand which has become legendary for its heroism they were forced to surrender.

It can be seen in retrospect that the failure of Market-Garden precluded the possibility of ending the war in 1944. But at the time heroism and optimism were paramount in everybody's mind. The scattering of the German forces made the conclusion of the war seem a virtual reality. Even the surprising enemy resistance at Arnhem seemed to register in Allied minds as no more than a flash in the pan. The lessons so painfully learned in Italy and elsewhere seemed to be forgotten. Even Eisenhower, relying on Intelligence reports of the crumbling of the German army, appears to have had a fuddled view of the general situation. Only Patton was concerned with 'keeping on the move, ferreting out the Hun, and trampling him into the dust.'

Characteristically, Patton had sneered at Montgomery's promotion to Field Marshal on 1 September: 'The Field Marshal thing made us sick, that is Bradley and me'; and Bradley uncharacteristically gave Bedell Smith his opinion that Montgomery was 'a third-rate General and he never did anything or won any battle that any other General

Below: Eisenhower handled even the difficult Montgomery with tact and diplomacy.

Left: Eisenhower talks to Sergeant McDavid of the 29th Division on the front on 14 11 1944.

command and the keen sense of urgency that informed the singular plans of General George Patton. Of the commanders he alone fitted his plans to the prevailing circumstances and not *vice versa*. In one of his less aggressive moods he put the matter in a nutshell: 'I think the difference between success and failure in high command depends upon the ability, or lack of it, to do just that.' There is evidence enough that from the end of August onward he tried by every possible means to urge a

Below: Eisenhower with Patton, the most forceful and aggressive of Eisenhower's generals.

could not have won as well or better.' Even Smith, for whom diplomacy was the watchword, accused Montgomery of 'intransigence and behind-the-scenes conniving to enhance his own prestige and to obtain a major measure of the command.'

The sneers, however, were not made manifest till long after the war was over. At the time, public opinion was formed on footage gained or lost in the battle; and the last quarter of the year was notable not only for the knives the Generals were raising to plunge into each other's backs but for the contrasted attitudes of *laissez-faire* that pervaded the attitudes of the lower echelons of

Below: Toward the end of the war Eisenhower's job of keeping both the Americans and British happy became more difficult.

Left: Eisenhower on a visit to a hospital in North Wales. Allied medical facilities were of high standard.

Below left: Eisenhower talks to a Canadian soldier while visiting Montgomery at his headquarters.

on the golf course at Rheims the Supreme Commander was necessarily playing. Since the course was covered with numerous tents and buildings that were part of headquarters it simply was impossible to play, so the story is totally unfounded. But around November there was general alarm that so little progress was being made, and Brooke was trying to drum up every possible excuse for taking power out of Eisenhower's hands. To be sure, an offensive ordered by Eisenhower in October had failed except for the capture of Metz. As one historian put it: 'The weather was appalling, ammunition ran short, and, after a fortnight's struggle in drenched fields and quagmires in which an advance of only eight miles was achieved at the point of greatest penetration, the Siegfried Line [the Western Wall] remained unbreached.' But Brooke's criticism of Eisenhower rarely slackened, and his diaries are peppered with niggling comments that are unworthy of him.

When at last the first German city, Aachen, was captured by General Joe Collins after fanatical resistance there was a gloss of triumph on the sustained attitude of torpor and an implied comment that in a few days the main prize, Berlin, would fall into Allied hands.

Eisenhower himself had his head in the clouds of victory. He raised no objection when on 15 December Montgomery told him he would like to be in England for Christmas as 'the enemy is at present fighting a defensive action on all fronts [and] his situation is such that he cannot stage major offensive operations.' Eisenhower too would have liked to go home. Mamie, presumably with Kay Summersby in mind, had been accusing him of 'dirty tricks' and pleading with him in letters to see that their son John, now a platoon commander with 71st Infantry Division, was kept out of harm's way. He replied, 'You've always put your own interpretation on every act, look or word of mine, and when you've made yourself unhappy, that has, in turn, made me the same. It's true we've now

concerted effort by the Allies. But they persisted in consolidating everything, in spreading themselves out as the Germans fled and Brussels, Dieppe, Boulogne, Calais, Bruges, Ghent, Charlesroi, Mons, Liége and Luxembourg, were liberated. With a completely unexpected suddenness the enemy appeared to have collapsed and no one except Patton, and to a lesser extent Montgomery, realized the wisdom of reinforcing success and leaving failure to take care of itself. Instead, having captured the port of Antwerp and thereby improved the supply position there was a general settling into a mood of torpor, of enjoying the fruits of victory in a quiet winter while on the eastern front the Russians were battering the enemy into submission and in the Far East MacArthur was 'island hopping' and the brilliant British commander

General Slim was methodically overcoming the Japanese offensive. 'All over bar the shouting' seemed to be an opinion shared by the British and American press. 'Ike goes golfing' was a favorite expression. The implication that Eisenhower was playing golf instead of attending to his job has become embedded in the mythology of the war. It arose from one of Brooke's diary entries:

'I put before the [Chief of Staff's] Committee my views on the very unsatisfactory state of affairs in France, with no one running the land battle. Eisenhower, though supposed to be doing so, is on the golf links at Rheims – entirely detached and taking no part in the running of the war.'

This jump to conclusions was based entirely on the CIGS's assumption that because Eisenhower's headquarters was

Left: Eisenhower with high-ranking Canadian officers during a visit to First Canadian Army.

been apart for two and a half years, and at a time and under conditions that make separations painful and hard to bear. Because you don't have a specific war job that absorbs your time and thoughts, I understand also that this distress is harder for you to bear. But you should not forget that I do miss you and do love you, and that the load of responsibility I carry would be intolerable unless I could have the belief that there is someone who wants me to come home – for good. Don't forget that I take a beating every day. . . . So far as John is concerned, we can do nothing

but pray. If I interfered even slightly or indirectly he would be so resentful for the remainder of his life. . . . Please try to see me in something besides a despicable light – and at least let me be *certain* of my welcome home when this mess is finished.'

As it was, neither Montgomery nor Eisenhower went home. Hitler took a hand. He was ill, wobbling and trembling from the effects of syphilis in its tertiary stage, able to walk only with the aid of a stick and entirely dependent on drugs prescribed by his head physician, Dr Theo Morell. But his mind was directed

fanatically toward a single aim: a new and final offensive that would cut off Montgomery's forces and in so doing isolate the Americans in the area where they were weakest – the Ardennes. When his Generals told him he had not the military strength for such an offensive he ranted on about 'dealing a few heavy blows that will cause the coalition to collapse like a great thunderclap.' His confused thinking embraced the day four years earlier when in the same area his forces had overcome the feeble French resistance in a few hours.

His inspiration was not without a certain credibility. There were only four divisions guarding the Ardennes, none of them strong in armor. Hitler scraped together the better part of 28 divisions, 10 of them armored. These he formed into the Sixth SS Panzer Army and the Fifth Panzer Army. His gasoline supply position was desperate, but by having it centralized and stored in underground dumps that would be proof against any bomb attacks by Allied air forces he reckoned he could keep the two Armies going for six weeks. In that time the tables could be turned. It was a gamble that depended on surprise, the weather, and no further demands for reinforcements for the Eastern Front. Those

Below: Eisenhower did not hear of Hitler's final attack, the Battle of the Bulge, for several hours.

needs granted, he had a fair chance. Two of the American divisions spread thinly across the Ardennes were wholly in-experienced and the others had suffered heavy casualties. His Intelligence brought him news of the Allies' smug self-satisfaction as they paused for Christ-mas revels and the final push through Germany to Berlin; and the meteorolo-gists saw little but snow, low cloud and rain. That left surprise. By limiting the dissemination of plans as much as possible to conferences and relying on landlines rather than radio for coded messages he thought secrecy could be maintained – as indeed it was. On the morning of 16 December, he struck.

On that day Eisenhower was attending the wedding of his batman, Mickey McKeogh, to a WAC Sergeant called Pearlie Hargrave in, of all places, the Louis XIV chapel at Versailles. Mont-gomery was playing golf with the pro-fessional Dai Rees at Eindhoven. There was general elation everywhere, not least because the United States Senate, not to be outmarshalled in the field of promotions, had created for their Supreme Commander a new five-star rank, General of the Army, so that Eisenhower should not seem to lag behind Montgomery's three-months-old rank of Field Marshal.

The news of the Ardennes counter-attack did not reach Eisenhower's head-quarters at Versailles until late in the afternoon of the 16th. By then, nearly 1000 tanks and armored assault guns had broken through the Ardennes front and reached a point 20 miles inside the Allied lines. A further complication was caused by the Germans' infiltration of a small number of captured American vehicles. These were used by highly trained English-speaking commandos in American uniforms who cut telephone wires, resited road signs, and erected notices indicating nonexistent minefields. When this ploy was discovered every genuine American immediately became suspect, causing farcical complications for the Security Police, who had no idea how many of these saboteurs' vehicles might have infiltrated. Then a rumor was spread that an 'assassination party' of disguised Germans had got through and were heading for Versailles, where they intended to kill Eisenhower. This resulted in the Supreme Com-mander being taken into custody by his own police and protected night and day by an armed guard. He was furious.

All this confusion naturally caused delays in the movement of traffic. In his *A Soldier's Story*, Bradley tells how 'a half-million GIs played cat and mouse with each other each time they met on the road.' They were forced to challenge everyone with questions that supposedly only an American could answer. Bradley himself was called upon by sentries to name the capital of Illinois, the name of Betty Grable's current husband and the name of a baseball player. Even he knew nothing of Miss Grable's spouse, so it may be imagined how poorly British liaison officers fared when challenged to prove their Allied status by answering such esoteric test questions.

The ultimate object of Hitler's daring offensive was to cause another Dunkirk by cutting off the Allied armies from their bases of supply. The Sixth SS Panzer Army was to strike northeast, cross the Meuse between Liège and Huy and sweep on to Antwerp. The Fifth Panzer Army, according to its commander, Manteuffel, 'was to ad-vance along a more curving line, cross the Meuse between Namur and Dinant, and push toward Brussels – to cover the flank.'

Left: The 101st Airborne move out of Bastogne during the siege that marked the turn of the battle.

Above left: Two tired defenders of Bastogne before the siege was lifted on 26 December 1944.

The group commander of the two Armies was Field Marshal Model but the executive planner of the operation was General Jodl of OKW. Manteuffel tells us that, 'Jodl had assured us there would be sufficient [gasoline] to develop our full strength and carry our drive through. This assurance proved completely mistaken. Part of the trouble was that OKW worked on a mathematical and stereotyped calculation of the amount . . . required to move a division for a hundred kilometers. My experience in Russia had taught me that double this scale was really needed under battlefield conditions. Jodl didn't understand this.'

What also had been forgotten – or perhaps entrusted too firmly to good fortune – was that the weather that so hamstrung the Allied air forces in bombing the German supply columns in the first days of the offensive also hindered the Luftwaffe when, on 23 December, the fog and low cloud cleared away and they found themselves to be vastly outnumbered and unable to protect the ground forces. In retrospect it can be seen that Hitler's offensive, brilliant though it was in conception, lost its impetus after the first week.

On the Allies' side during that first week the elation generated by the Versailles wedding and the thought of Christmas and victory died slowly and with reluctance. Various soothing phrases such as 'Let them come' and 'It's only a

Above: Supreme Allied Commander Eisenhower in Europe during one of his frequent tours.

Below: Eisenhower sporting five stars. He was made General of the Army on 15 December 1944.

spoiling attack' were mixed up with the alarms and excursions. It was bitterly cold, snow encrusted the hills and forested plateau, fog prevented the use of Allied aircraft. The swift advance of the German armor seemed incredible. Although forced into a bottleneck the tanks rolled on until they ran out of oil and ammunition, the Allied dumps they had hoped to capture having been blown up before being seized. They managed to get within siege distance of Bastogne and called upon the commander of the 101st Airborne Division, dug in there, to surrender. His name, Brigadier General Anthony McAuliffe, became famous for the succinct reply given to the surrender call: 'Nuts!'

Meuse was the utmost distance to which Hitler's Generals could push their troops. Allied torpor gave way to brilliant strategy in the nick of time, with Eisenhower handing over command in the northern area to Montgomery, who later claimed to have saved the situation; but it was Patton who relieved Bastogne, having hurled no fewer than 133,000 vehicles into action without adequate supplies of oil to keep them going. He told his men to 'get out and walk' when they could get no farther. At home, Brooke the CIGs rumbled away in a series of telegrams to Montgomery that Eisenhower was ignorant of the situation and should – indeed must – hand over command to Montgomery. Churchill was embroiled to give his imprimatur to the change and

further telegrams were exchanged with lightning speed. But by that time Eisenhower had made the change anyway. 'The CIGs,' Eisenhower told Smith, 'has this idea that he's the only one capable of the power of thought.' But Brooke's biographer, Sir Arthur Bryant, adds a gracenote to Brooke's more or less continuously spiteful attitude to Eisenhower's command:

'Nor in the hour of crisis was the Supreme Commander unworthy of the men he led. Calamity acted on Eisenhower like a restorative and brought out all the greatness in his character. It was he who, as soon as the news of defeat reached him, overruled Bradley, halted the offensive south of the Moselle, and ordered Patton to march north against the Germans' flank; who threw in the two airborne divisions – his sole reserve – to hold Bastogne and the Meuse crossings; who opened a conference of his senior commanders with the words "I want only cheerful faces," and declared that the situation should be regarded as one not of disaster, but opportunity. His Order of the Day – comparable to Haig's "Backs to the Wall" Order of 1918 – contained the prophecy, "By rushing out from his fixed defenses the enemy has given us the chance to turn his gamble into his worst defeat."'

So it turned out. Hitler had had a brilliant idea that, as his Generals had warned him, he was incapable of implementing. However, without doubt he had dealt the Allies a blow. The Americans alone had lost 70,000 men and the war had been drawn out into a new year – though there had never been any solidly-based hope that it would end in 1944. Also during the early days of 1945, when the Allies were delivering effective counterstrokes to ensure that Hitler was not only crushed but beaten into the ground too, there was a final small fizzle in the form of a German firecracker aimed at Strasbourg, which was held by the French as well as some American troops Eisenhower needed for his final blows at Hitler. As Supreme Commander he ordered the evacuation of the city. De Gaulle countermanded Eisenhower's order and told the French to stand firm, which they did, and held the city. True, De Gaulle had persuaded Eisenhower reluctantly to agree 'for political reasons'; but in effect it stood

Left: US infantry fire from the cover of a water-side restaurant during the final push into Germany.

Below left: US troops shelter from German fire under a railroad tunnel on 11 March 1945.

forward so fast that their advance troops were within 40 miles of Berlin by mid-February. At the same time Harris's bomber squadrons were over Dresden, which was full of refugees fleeing from the Russians. The city was razed to the ground and the Germans claimed that 250,000 had been killed – though perhaps a tenth of that number would be the true figure.

It was clear to all in that first quarter of 1945 that the armies of the Third Reich were finished, and that the so-called 'thousand-year Reich' itself had collapsed around the forces that had propped it up. The first official surrender was by the German forces in Italy, who capitulated on 29 April and signed themselves away on 2 May. Between the capitulation and the actual signing of the surrender document Hitler shot himself on 30 April, having handed the reins of office to Admiral Dönitz, who made a muddled attempt to surrender to Eisenhower without completing a similar surrender to the Soviet Union. Eisenhower was having none of that, and said so. On 4 May Field Marshal Wilhelm Keitel, a sycophantic yes-man from the remnants of the German High Command, surrendered

as a countermand to the order of the highest luminary. The French-American relationship had never been cordial and both Eisenhower and De Gaulle were going to nurse grievances over this as over other things; but Churchill, who had learned about Strasbourg during a visit to Eisenhower's forward headquarters at St Germains, saw Eisenhower's reluctant agreement as 'gentlemanly' and De Gaulle's stiffnecked acceptance as 'gratitude.' Kay Summersby wrote in her diary, 'E. tries to please too many people.'

In January 1945 the Soviet armies began a tremendous offensive that swept

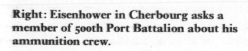

Right: Eisenhower in Cherbourg asks a member of 500th Port Battalion about his ammunition crew.

Above: Eisenhower visits the XVI Corps area to check the progress in crossing the Rhine.

to Montgomery the German forces in Holland, North Germany, Schleswig-Holstein, Denmark, the Friesian Islands and Heligoland; and to Eisenhower the occupation forces in Norway who had never raised a hand in anger. Jodl, Keitel's junior but more aggressive colleague, signed an unconditional surrender at Eisenhower's headquarters at Rheims on 7 May. Next day he had to sign again in Berlin because the Soviet Union would not accept what they referred to as a 'subordinate' surrender; but Eisenhower had already sent his formal telegram to the Chiefs of Staff advising them of Victory in Europe: 'The mission of the Allied Force was fulfilled at 0241, local time, May 7th, 1945.' VE Day was celebrated by Britain and the United States on 8 May, and by the Soviet Union, making an issue of the delay, on 9 May.

In *Eisenhower as Military Commander* Major General Eric Sixsmith sums up Eisenhower's soldierly qualities:

'We are left with the picture of a commander of manifest integrity who warmed the heart and uplifted the spirit of everyone who worked with him. His special genius was skill at management. He managed the Generals, the Admirals and the Air Marshals, and even the politicians, and he managed mighty armies. One special facet of this quality was his ability to draw the best from those under him, to draw from them and not steal the praise. His own heart and mind were with the fighting men, and

his preference would have been to command in the forefront of the battle. But that was not to be his destiny or his *métier*. His task was to weld together a force which was not only an Allied force but one drawn from all services, and to direct it so that its whole weight was used most effectively to the single aim of the defeat of the common enemy. That he did superbly.'

This seems a fair encomium, but on the debit side it must be added that Eisenhower was often overcautious in directing his battles. He was much given to reining in the efforts of his most brilliant commanders, Patton and Bradley, to outwit the Germans. In consequence the Germans never failed to seize opportunities that brought them minor victories when they were outgunned or outnumbered. Also, Eisenhower's management skill was to a great extent dependent on staff who sometimes failed him in their exercise of tact – the quality which above all was necessary in the manipulations of the commander of a mighty army. Harry Butcher was one such, who, by being too free with the confidences he had recorded and the notes which Eisenhower himself had committed to paper and which Butcher ferreted out from the War Department files, did no good at all to the prickly relationships that existed among the leaders of the ironically named United Nations. Diplomatic though he was, Eisenhower was no different from anyone else in speaking his mind, especially when he believed he was talking in confidence, about those whose conduct or personal characteristics irritated him. But as was to be proved he had attached too much faith to the description 'confidential aide' when he had appointed Butcher to be the recorder of his occasional outbursts

Below: Eisenhower inspects a deadly German weapon while on a tour of the Third Army front.

of animosity. Butcher tended to be a trumpet rather than a sounding board and after the war published diary entries in the *Saturday Evening Post* which caused great embarrassment and had to be watered down, insofar as they could be, by many apologetic letters from Eisenhower to Montgomery, Churchill, MacArthur, Admiral King and others. Churchill put Butcher in his place in his acknowledgment to Eisenhower: 'Great events and personalities are made small when passed through the medium of this small mind,' and Eisenhower with uncharacteristic glumness told Sergeant Mickey McKeogh, 'I'm knackered.'

He was not of course. He had only been shown to have occasional uncharitable thoughts, which surprised those who had known him only as a wizard diplomat who had always contrived to create harmony where there was previously discord. But the surprise

Above left: Standing by a gallows, Eisenhower hears of atrocities from occupants of a former concentration camp.

Left: Eisenhower talks to just one of 40,000 American prisoners of war awaiting transportation home.

Below left: Eisenhower converses with a German POW who is awaiting transportation to the US.

Below: Eisenhower watches as the Unconditional Surrender documents are signed by the Allies and the Germans.

Top: Eisenhower and Mayor La Guardia surrounded by an exuberant crowd as they leave City Hall, New York.

Center: Eisenhower is reunited with his mother after a long parting at Kansas City Airport.

Far right, top: Eisenhower, with Churchill, pauses a moment outside the Guild Hall in London. He was given the freedom of the city.

Far right, center: Eisenhower and Tedder salute the crowds with broad smiles in a euphoric postwar London.

Right: A parade in honor of Eisenhower in New York City. Eisenhower always attracted huge and excited crowds.

Left: As part of his triumphant return home, Eisenhower addresses a joint session of Congress on 18 6 1945.

Center left: Eisenhower with his wife and son. He visited New York, Kansas City and his home town, Abilene, Kansas.

Bottom left: Allied leaders in front of their new headquarters after the first meeting of the Allied Control Council.

Right: General De Gaulle pins the French Medal of Liberation to Eisenhower's jacket at the Arc de Triomph.

was short-lived. Eisenhower's stature was in no way diminished by his having been shown to have frailties as well as strengths. He was, after all, a very human being.

On the other side of the world the war against Japan continued unabated. Burma was recaptured by the British in May, but the Japanese continued to fight with bitter ferocity, knowing only too well that they faced economic collapse. The British and United States navies had made an end of most of Japan's merchant shipping and supplies of raw materials and food were at rock bottom. The American air forces attacked Japanese cities ceaselessly. The Prime Minister, Admiral Suzuki, who

had fought in the Russo–Japanese war, urged the government to seek peace 'while it could still be sought with honor.' There was no way of saving face, for it was obvious that the Allies would insist on unconditional surrender just as they had with Germany. Unconditional surrender would bring about a revolt in the armed forces, for it did not lie within their comprehension. Also, the Imperial Dynasty must continue at all costs.

The Allied leaders met at Potsdam in July and decided to call upon Japan to surrender. No surrender was forthcoming; but exploratory feelers came from the Emperor Hirohito himself, who sent envoys to Moscow to negotiate for peace – one of them Prince Konoye, whom he told to accept peace 'at any price.' It was clear that Japan was a defeated nation, with only the militaristic heads of the army and navy holding out for some face-saving clause in the surrender terms. It was equally clear that very little more time would be needed to force Japan to cease fighting

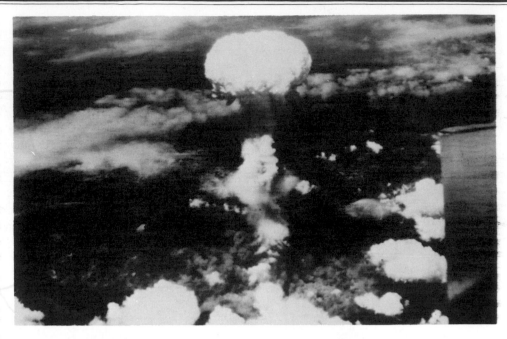

Above right: Smoke billows up from Nagasaki after the second atom bomb has been dropped on Japan on 9 August 1945.

Right: A 'Fat Man' bomb of the type dropped on Nagasaki. Eisenhower opposed the decision to use nuclear weapons against Japan.

Below: Japanese members of the surrender commission sign the peace treaty in deathly silence. MacArthur stands to the left.

if not actually to surrender. This the Allies knew. But they – specifically the United States – had an untried weapon with which American and British scientists had been experimenting for three years. This was the atomic bomb, a device for delivering a controlled nuclear explosion, and Truman, who had succeeded Roosevelt when he died in April, wanted to quicken the end of the war by using it against Japan without prior warning. Marshall agreed with him. Eisenhower believed that it was completely unnecessary 'to hit them with that dreadful thing.' Some scientists, in particular Professor James Franck, advised the US government that 'the military advantages and the saving of American lives achieved by the sudden use of atomic bombs against Japan may be outweighed by a wave of horror and repulsion spreading over the rest of the world.' He went on to a further warning: 'If the United States were to be the first to release this new means of indiscriminate destruction on mankind, she would sacrifice public support throughout the world, precipitate the race for armaments, and prejudice the possibility of reaching an international agreement on the future control of such weapons.'

As the historian Liddell Hart says, 'It was the scientists who were closest to the statesmen's ears [who] had a

better chance of gaining attention, and their eager arguments prevailed in the decision.' After the first of the three bombs the Americans had manufactured was test exploded in Alamogordo, New Mexico, on 16 July and found to be successful, it was agreed that the cities of Hiroshima and Nagasaki should be targets – 'this time for real,' as Eisenhower put it with suppressed horror – for the other two.

On Monday 6 August a B-29 Superfortress called *Enola Gay*, piloted by Colonel Tibbets, released the first atomic bomb over Hiroshima. It had been nicknamed 'Little Boy,' and it devastated an area nearly 50 square miles in extent. Some 80,000 people were instantly killed and 40,000 injured. The

Above: Marines of the USS *Missouri* stand to attention as the Japanese Mission leaves after the surrender ceremony.

number who subsequently suffered from radiation has never been determined. President Truman joyfully declared that the bomb was 'the greatest thing in history'; and because the members of the Japanese cabinet who remained opposed to unconditional surrender still refused to give in, Truman authorized the release of the second bomb, named 'Fat Man,' over Nagasaki. Furthermore, though the stock of atomic bombs was now exhausted, he promised the Japanese a 'rain of ruin' if they still refused to give in. Neither the Emperor, Admiral Suzuki, nor any of their advisers knew whether the threat could be implemented or not; but the Emperor was not prepared to go any further. On 14 August he told his indecisive parliament: 'If nobody else has any opinion to express, we would express our own. We demand that you will agree to it. We see only one way for Japan to save herself. That is the reason we have made this determination to endure the unendurable and suffer the insufferable.' Japan then surrendered, though Truman graciously agreed that the dynasty of emperors should be preserved in Hirohito's sacred person. The document was signed by MacArthur and Hirohito's representative aboard USS *Missouri* in Tokyo Bay on 2 September. Pearl Harbor had been avenged, 'the day of infamy matched,' as MacArthur put it. World War II was over.

Below: The devastation at Nagasaki finally persuaded the Japanese to surrender and brought peace to the East.

8: DISCORD

There was discord abounding in the immediate postwar period. There were bitter arguments about the division of Berlin into zones controlled by Britain, France, the Soviet Union and the United States – although there was little sense in laying down demarcation lines in a ruined city that had ceased to be the seat of the Nazi government. Greed and egotism, rather than common sense, prevailed and in retrospect the so-called United Nations can be seen quarrelling like alley cats over the spoils of a ruined continent.

From this bitter conflict Eisenhower stood aloof in spirit even though it was not possible to stand aloof in practical terms; for the battle had now become political. The phrase 'unconditional surrender' gave rise to perplexity when the Allies, recalling the trouble it had caused when implemented in absurdly impracticable terms of revenge after World War I, tried to ameliorate it with what were loosely called 'justice and mercy.' Those Christian qualities proved to be just as elusive when it came to exercising them. The leading Nazis and camp followers who had not escaped and gone to ground were brought to book in the Nuremberg War Crimes Trial that was set up in November 1945 and lasted until October 1946. Varying degrees of complicity in what were called variously 'war crimes,' 'crimes against peace' and 'crimes against humanity' brought sentences ranging from 10 years' imprisonment to death on the 177 men and women who were found guilty – only three were acquitted.

Suddenly among the Western Allies there arose suspicions that the Russians were trying to claim more than their fair share of the spoils and fears that Stalin's infinitely larger forces might make possession nine points of the law if it came to renewed conflict – this time between East and West. Some of the difficulty was caused by the new President of the United States, Harry S Truman, who as Vice President had succeeded Roosevelt when he died in April. Truman was without much political experience, did not like the Russians, and did not trouble to seem – or indeed to be – cooperative in dealing with them. He scorned their losses of 20,000,000 dead, which as the President of a huge nation that lost only 300,000, was not very tactful, and talked about 'taking up the cudgels' for American rights when it came to reparations. The Soviet Union ignored him and took a chunk of East Prussia for themselves, causing much huffing and puffing among the Western Allies. But Churchill had told the House of Commons that 'Marshal Stalin and the Soviet Leaders wish to live in honorable friendship and equality with the western democrats,' so the trifling matter of a somewhat uncertain Polish frontier was swept under the carpet. It remained there until 28 years later, when the frontier was acknowledged by the West German State to be in existence precisely where the Soviet Union had put it. Looking back, it seems that except for the absence of gunfire and bombing the continent of Europe was not a very peaceful place in 1945's latter half. 'A cauldron,' Eisenhower told Mamie. 'I am playing as much golf as possible.'

Reasonably enough, Eisenhower thought he had earned his retirement; but 'late in 1945,' he writes in *Mandate for Change,* 'I was ordered back to the United States and assigned as Chief of Staff of the United States Army. When I reported to the White House, the President was aware of my desire to retire, but I was naturally appreciative of the honor implied in his decision. Chief of Staff of the Army was a position that, prior to World War II, would probably have been, because of my age in grade and the vagaries of promotion and retirement laws, completely beyond my reach; though then it would have seemed challenging and interesting. But to me in 1945, returning to the United States only a few months after Hitler's destruction and having lived through years of war's excitement, drama, and never-ending anxieties, the prospect of directing the tedious job of Army demobilization – particularly in the light of my belief that unilateral disarmament on such a preci-

Right: Eisenhower appears on nationwide television after a visit to Europe as Supreme Allied Commander, Europe.

Above: Göring, Hess, Ribbentrop, Dönitz, Raeder and Schirach at the Nuremburg War Crimes Trial.

Left: The Nuremburg trials were controversial, but of the 177 men and women who stood trial, only three were acquitted.

pitate, helter-skelter basis was unwise – was frankly distasteful. But responding to the President's suggestion that I serve as Chief of Staff until General Omar Bradley could be released from his assignment in the Veterans Administration, I was ready to report for duty at any date he desired. The President thought that, on this basis, I would serve for about two years. My hope of retirement was, though not destroyed, for this period deferred. I took over General George C. Marshall's responsibilities in December 1945.'

It was as he said a boring job. The office of Chief of Staff of the Army comes to life only during preparations for war, in the course of the war itself and in the subsequent slowing down of activities. Unwinding the army can justly be said to be the least exciting of the office's three active phases. However Eisenhower found its routines engaging if not exciting. The political and economic situations were totally different from those prevailing in the early 1920s. The

advances in technology caused largely by the demands of total war had created facilities that in turn had had their effect on consumer demand for what had once been 'luxury' goods. Expanding prosperity meant that there were more jobs than workers to fill them; and Truman's 'GI Bill of Rights' gave solidly based seniority rights to mustered-out soldiers, plus college education, job reinstatement, subsidies for the establishment of businesses, loans for the purchasing of homes and guaranteed pay for at least the one year of a 'settling down' period. Thus cushioned, and with a competent Civil Service to administer the laws, men and women were discharged from the services with the speed of light. In less than a year 9,000,000 were mustered out and rehabilitated. Eisenhower oversaw the transition from Parnassan height and could hardly have been said to be overworked. He was called upon for far more than his Washington post demanded. Many great business corporations sought his advice in solving their administrative problems and numerous social organizations begged him to address them on any subject he cared to choose. In the private side of his life he and Mamie gradually renewed the bonds of affection that had been so severely tested during the war years. Golf, bridge, poker and the reading of Westerns and 'comics' provided all the leisure activities he needed, though he recognized that he was 'getting paunchier' – perhaps because cutting his cigarette intake from 80 to 40 a day improved his appetite. It is worth noting as an idiosyncrasy that during his frequent visits to England, he refused invitations to formal luncheons and dinners because of the custom of not smoking until after the Loyal Toast had been drunk. To accommodate him at one formal dinner to which it would have been virtually lese-majesty to refuse an invitation, the Chairman, Mountbatten, brought the Loyal Toast forward to the soup course. Traditionalists vented their disapproval in the columns of the press.

Though he never openly sought popularity by building up a great public relations organization, Eisenhower was a natural folk hero. There were those who said that his reluctance to publicize himself was a subtle way of encouraging the limelight; but be that as it may, he continually and modestly disabused people of the notion of heroism that clung to him, emphasizing the rarity of the opportunities he had had to be 'in' the battle rather than directing it. 'With your battle headquarters sometimes as much as four hundred miles behind the front-line GI,' he said, 'you're four hundred times less of a hero than he is.' But the more he shed assumptions of glamor the more his hayseed modesty (most cogently expressed in the strip-cartoon balloon phrase 'Aw, shucks!) was treated as a kind of glamor in itself. He was GI Joe Doakes in the uniform of a General of the Army, straddling the gap between the man in the street and the great leader and beaming on everyone with naive astonishment that wherever he went 'We like Ike' posters were displayed in welcome. When he spoke in public about the great men with and under whom he had served – the government leaders, the naval, military and air commanders, the Chiefs of Staff and the men of eminence in science – they were all 'great fellers' and the jokes were all against himself. His indiscretions revealed in private diaries he had trusted others to keep private, and the inevitable debunkings that trickled out in the memoirs of those who saw his faults and took a delight in displaying them under the guise of 'straight talk,' brought little opprobrium down on him from the heights of public popularity. 'Rightly or wrongly, pinches of salt were cast upon such publications,' he notes with innocent surprise. He need

Below: Eisenhower's first glimpse of postwar Japan is on a visit to confer with General MacArthur.

Above: Eisenhower enjoying a break from his somewhat monotonous duties as General of the Army in postwar America.

Below: A carefully posed shot of General of the Army, Dwight D Eisenhower, taken in November 1947.

not have been surprised. All great men are allowed their peccadilloes, which are proof that they are only human after all.

While Eisenhower stuck gamely to the mixed blessings of the Chief of Staff's job, his colleague Omar Bradley plowed the furrow of Administrator of Veteran Affairs – a task for which he was even less suited than was Eisenhower for peacetime Chief of Staff, though both men had the character that turned the dutiful into the opportune. In February 1948 Bradley completed his term of office in Veteran Affairs and, according to plan, succeeded Eisenhower as Chief of Staff. 'I can now shed my uniform and become plain Ike Eisenhower with no service responsibilities,' he wrote to his brother Milton. He was talking lightly, as he knew very well. As a General of the Army he was in theory on active service for life, receiving the pay and allowances of his rank, and could be mustered at any time. However, retirement in the practical sense was of course allowed and it began with a long spell of terminal leave. During that time he was invited by the syndics of Columbia University to become its President – 'An invitation that I found most flattering, since I could lay no claim to any but the most ordinary education outside the military sphere.'

Some harsh critics said at the time that he was elected only because many voters among the syndics confused him with Milton, who was a distinguished academic; and the satirists among the entertainers of the decade made great play with his supposed inability to understand academic matters. Others said that the Presidency of Columbia was a convenient escape from the office of Chief of Staff at a time when demobilization seemed to have no place among the increasing tensions of the Cold War. It is possible that there was a certain

Left: Eisenhower meets the press in civilian clothes following his retirement as US Army Chief of Staff.

amount of substance behind these observations.

Eisenhower's predecessors in the Presidency – especially Nicholas Murray Butler – had gradually raised the status of Columbia from that of a small college to that of one of the leading universities in the Union, incorporating schools of law, architecture, political science, philosophy, pure science, medicine and many other disciplines. 'It was very proudly that I accepted the appointment. I felt it to be very suitable for a dignified but not inactive retirement.'

As well it may have been. Eisenhower scarcely had the chance to find out. Another and even greater dignity was being prepared for his consideration.

The first Eisenhower had heard of the possibility of his being invited to run for President was in 1943, when Virgil Pinkley, a newspaper correspondent covering the North African Theater and interviewing the Supreme Commander about his sweeping success in clearing North Africa of Hitler's forces, had reminded him that it was almost certain that with his experience of commanding and planning enterprises of such magnitude he would be considered a strong nominee for the Presidency. Were there not an ample number of precedents for such a nomination? Pinkley instanced Washington, Jackson, Harrison, Taylor and Grant, all of whom had been voted into the Presidency largely because of their successful control of large military forces and their administrative ability.

General Patton, who as we know ran hot and cold in his admiration for Eisenhower, says that on hearing Pinkley's hint there was a response that to Patton meant 'Ike wants to be President so badly you can taste it.' Eisenhower says he laughed the idea off. A great traditionalist, he had little love for politics, which he found tedious, or for the devious ways of politicians. His love of tradition was based on a homelier premise – the one about which he reminded his brother Milton, who in 1943 had become President of Kansas State College: 'Good, oldfashioned patriotism.' Pinkley's comment was deflected with one of Eisenhower's simple jokes, 'Virgil,' he said, 'you've been standing out in the sun too long.'

If he could scorn the hint of a newsman he could hardly adopt the same attitude to the President himself, and when Truman rode with him through the American zone of Berlin after Germany's surrender in 1945 he said with complete earnestness that he would aid Eisenhower to attain any height he liked to aim at, including the Presidency.

If scorn was possible, certainly respectful disbelief was: 'I doubt that any soldier of our country was ever so suddenly struck in his emotional vitals by a President with such an apparently

Below: Eisenhower with the Standing Group of the North Atlantic Treaty Organization after visiting European NATO members.

sincere and certainly astounding proposition as this. . . . To have the President suddenly throw this broadside into me left me no recourse except to treat it as a very splendid joke, which I hoped it was. I laughed heartily and said: "Mr President, I don't know who will be your opponent for the Presidency, but it will not be I."'

Whether or not the respectful disbelief was false modesty in diguise is a matter for conjecture. But on the face of it Eisenhower was not playing hard to get: he claims he simply did not want to become embroiled in state affairs, which he 'had long come to the conclusion'

Below: Eisenhower helped to set up NATO as a defensive peace organization while MacArthur fought in Korea.

were outside either his interest or his abilities. When, on his appointment as Chief of Staff, he found himself in closer touch with Congress and Senate than he had ever been, and therefore apparently more politically available, he found talk about the Presidency so widespread and to him so tiresome, that he found his sense of humor was 'beginning to show signs of wear and tear' and drafted a handout with which he replied to press references to the possibility of his nomination for the 1948 elections. In it he mentioned the effrontery that would be ascribed to him if he assumed that any significant number of electors wanted him in any other field than the military, and concluded 'In any event, my decision to remove myself completely from the political scene is definite and positive.

I know you will not object to my making this letter public to inform all interested persons that I could not accept nomination even under the remote circumstances that it were tendered to me.'

For a time the letter was effective but as soon as he changed into the civilian status of the President of Columbia University there was an assumption that without a uniform he was available again. Walter Winchell the radio personality who commanded an audience of millions asked his listeners to send Eisenhower postcards urging him to accept the presidential nomination. They arrived at Columbia in truckloads and had to be dealt with by the Bureau of Applied Social Research, whose diligent researchers delightedly came to the conclusion that 97.3 per cent of the communicants were in favor of Eisenhower's nomination for the Presidency. He re-

Below: The Allies were stationed in Germany after the war as occupation forces, and later as NATO forces.

Above: Eisenhower reports to President Truman after visiting Europe to discuss the organization of NATO.

mained, however, adamant, though highly amused that the urgings were equally balanced between Republicans and Democrats. Playing bridge with Omar Bradley one night soon after Bradley had taken over the office of Chief of Staff, the new COS said, 'Goddam, Ike, they don't care what politics you are, you're their baby.' 'No bid,' Eisenhower said.

He was at Columbia for two and a half years. Although he was not anxious to put himself in the limelight he introduced and helped establish an enterprise called the American Assembly, encouraged a growing interest in the conservation of human resources and founded a Chair of Peace. His presidency of Columbia was cut short in December 1950, when Truman told him that the members of the North Atlantic Treaty Organization, founded in 1949 to organize collective defense among its member states, wanted him as their commander. Would he accept the appointment? 'Since I was still an officer in the army, I replied that if the President, as Commander-in-chief, felt that I could undertake the assignment with a better

armor, in Europe, and there were grave suspicions that the Cold War might warm up at any moment. It says much for the fatalistic attitude of the American people that they had accepted, with scarcely a demur, the abandonment of the precious Jeffersonian concept of no entangling alliances with other nations in peacetime and approved the North Atlantic Treaty. There had been no alliance with any other government since that with France in 1778. But as one of NATO's press officers was quick to note, an alliance was not much use without someone to shape it; and the word 'shape' made a punning acronym for

Right: Eisenhower on the steps of SHAPE headquarters with other high-ranking NATO members and British MPs.

Below right: It is perhaps ironic that while Eisenhower helped found NATO, MacArthur fought an aggressive war in Korea.

Above: General of the Army Eisenhower is greeted by General of the Army Bradley at MATS Terminal, National Airport.

Right: Eisenhower about to enter the Pentagon building on 5 11 1951 as SHAPE Commander.

chance of success than any other soldier of his choice, my affirmative answer was inevitable.'

Almost immediately Eisenhower departed for Europe, where he hurriedly toured the member countries to ensure that they really did want him again as Supreme Allied Commander – this time of peacetime forces – in Europe. There were no doubts expressed; nor was that surprising. The North Atlantic Treaty Organization belied its name: there was a treaty but little organization. What was needed was a leader and a system. The Cold War had brought the organization into being and its members were aghast when, with little more than a committee to put its tenets into practical form, the Soviet Union exploded 'an atomic device.' No longer had the Americans control of nuclear energy. There was widespread alarm and everybody began to talk about the recall to the colors of those who were only now beginning to enjoy the peace they had fought for. There was only one American infantry division, plus some token pieces of

Above left: Infantry troops watch for movement in a Communist-held region while UN troops drop white phosphorous.

Below left: Eisenhower's diplomatic and organizational talents were put to good use in establishing NATO.

Supreme Headquarters Allied Powers in Europe, which Eisenhower quickly established near Paris. Here once again, with the wide grin and the ability to 'manage' people so that temporary assuagement of their mutual enmities eased progress, was the country lad from Kansas resplendent in the uniform of a five-star general.

While he was setting NATO on its feet and winding up the machinery of defensive peace, his erstwhile boss in the Philippines, Douglas MacArthur, fighting a bitter war in Korea and trying desperately to avoid a situation such as the British had created for themselves by their *laissez-faire* policy in the Far East, was acting in an extremely aggressive

way. He wanted to bomb Manchuria and tie up with Chiang Kai-shek's armies in an all-out war with Red China, thus extending instead of containing the conflict which, like the Cold War in Europe, was not merely a threat to local peace but to world peace. Warned many times by Truman to keep control over his enthusiasm for dominating the Far East, he settled his own fate by challenging the Presidential right to aim for a negotiated peace, publicly announced 'There is no substitute for victory,' and defiantly threatened China with attack. Truman had had enough. He consulted with Secretary of Defense Marshall and Chief of Staff Bradley and dismissed MacArthur from his command. The glamorous General returned to America to receive the plaudits of a multitude who, largely as a consequence of MacArthur's own publicity machine, thought it a disgrace that he had been fired from a command that would have led to justified American domination of the Pacific and Asiatic Theaters. The commotion died

Above: Eisenhower receiving his fifth Distinguished Service Medal from President Truman after 40 years of service.

down, however, as it was gradually revealed that many of MacArthur's claims were exaggerated and that his continued involvement in the Far East would have meant, as Bradley observed, continuing to fight 'the wrong war, at the wrong place, at the wrong time, and with the wrong enemy.' The cautious approach of a man like Eisenhower was infinitely preferable at a time when most nations were shivering in the shoes of threatened peace. It was an irony that MacArthur, bone ignorant of politics but with an outsize ego that fed his longing to inhabit the White House, should cheer himself along to a Presidential campaign that failed lamentably to recapture his popularity while Eisenhower, more understanding of politics than he pretended but with no highflown aims in the direction of Washington, should find himself in the White House.

9: PRESIDENT

Truman's government of Democrats came to an end in 1952. It had encountered heavy weather. The rocks upon which the ship of state had nearly foundered had included: racial discrimination; the trial of Alger Hiss, which resulted in the Red Scare that gave rise to the activities of Senator Joseph McCarthy of Wisconsin; and the confession of Klaus Fuchs to having disclosed details of atomic bomb construction to the Soviet Union and the subsequent execution of his accomplices the Rosenbergs; the Cold War; and the Korean War. Truman's dismissal of MacArthur as a trade-in for peace negotiations in Korea restored something of his image as a great statesman, but with 130,000 American casualties to be counted against the Korean War there were considerably fewer takers for the Democratic ticket.

In such a climate the potential of a folk hero such as Eisenhower flourished. It was clear to all, as one historian says, that 'he displayed transparent honesty, integrity, prudence, a talent for mediating among men of diverse views, and the ability to inspire loyalty among subordinates and confidence among associates.' He was recognized as a figurehead rather than a chief executive with unlimited powers. It was plain from his past record that his genius was for getting along with almost everybody and offending as few people as possible – negative virtues to be sure, but in the prevailing circumstances eminently desirable. If he could be persuaded to come out from under the bushel where he modestly hid his cheery light he 'might not solve problems but . . . serve as a good-luck amulet to charm them away.'

It seemed that persuasion was no easy task. Eisenhower's professed interest in politics being minimal and his references to the subject virtually nil, it was not even known for certain whether he voted Republican or Democrat. Eventually he reluctantly conceded that he had always 'gone the Republican ticket' because his father had. Influential persuaders flew off to SHAPE headquarters in Paris to renew their efforts to entice him toward the splendors of the Presidency. Among them was Senator Henry Cabot Lodge, who gave him a lecture on the need for Republicans after 20 years of Democrats and concluded with ardor, 'You *must* permit the use of your name in the upcoming primaries.' Still Eisenhower held out against persuasion; but Lodge 'argued with the tenacity of a bulldog and pounded away on this theme until, as he left, I said I would "think the matter over."' It was not Lodge, however, or even the plea in a letter from Truman himself that, Eisenhower says, finally convinced him that his duty to the country lay in allowing himself to be nominated: it was a Miss Jacqueline Cochran, representing an organization called 'Citizens for Eisenhower,' who flew hotfoot into Paris bearing the copy of a film of a Madison Square Garden rally two days earlier, who switched his mind. The film showed 15,000 people who had gathered in the garden at the inconvenient time of midnight to endorse, by wild shouts and frantic waving of hats and flags, the view that Dwight D Eisenhower should be the thirty-third President of the United States.

'The incident,' he writes in *Mandate for Change*, 'impressed me more than all the arguments presented by the individuals who had been plaguing me with political questions for many months. When our guest departed, I think [Mamie and I] both suspected, although we did not say so, that our lives were to be once more uprooted.'

Eisenhower's inheritance at the White House was not an enviable one. Monetary inflation was causing industrial strangulation; McCarthyism was still rife; the solution to Korea had not been found; and, most damaging, the Republican candidate for the vice-presidency, Richard M Nixon of California, was alleged to have been accepting handouts to a private 'expenses' fund from businessmen in return for favors granted or promised. With an earnestness that proved to be as hollow as his later defense of himself in the murky Watergate case,

Right: Eisenhower exerting his well-known charm on some 75 gleeful first and second graders who have given him a golf hat.

Left: Ike becomes a strong candidate for nomination in the Republican Convention at Chicago on 8 11 1952.

Top: Nixon's daughter Julie was particularly impressed with the famous general she had heard so much about.

Above: Eisenhower acknowledges the cheers of the crowd after the biggest speech of his presidential campaign in Madison Square.

Nixon went on television complete with his family and the family dog, and pleaded with a nationwide audience to understand his innocence. His plea climbed the heights of skill in public relations when on the following evening he and Eisenhower appeared together for a campaign speech in West Virginia and Eisenhower embraced Nixon and murmured the words 'That's my boy.' He had evidently forgotten his mystification, expressed in his letter to Mamie back in 1929, with the processes of corruption in high places. Or perhaps, having chosen Nixon himself as the vice-presidential candidate, he was anxious to prove that he was always ready to see the best in people.

It was quite clear from the results of the election that the people saw the best in Eisenhower. He won an enormous victory over the Democratic candidate Adlai Stevenson, receiving 33,936,000 votes compared with Stevenson's 27,315,000. Almost immediately he went off to Korea, where he accomplished little but returned giving the impression that he was at least on the right side, that the good-luck charm was working. His choice of cabinet too seemed to be solidly and sensibly based on the notion of giving successful business men direction of the administrative and economic

resources of the country. As in the army, he wanted men he could delegate to and leave them to get on with whatever needed doing. Who better as a Secretary of State than a prominent Wall Street lawyer? John Foster Dulles fulfilled every requirement. Three high-powered executives from General Motors got key jobs in the cabinet, and one of them, Charles Wilson, immortalized himself in the quotation books by having said 'What's good for our country is good for General Motors, and vice versa.' It became clear very soon that the army 'staff' system to which Eisenhower was accustomed was going to be a boon to him as President. He did not mind working hard, but as in his youth he

Left: After visiting Korea, President-elect Eisenhower made a good-will tour of Honolulu. He is with Admiral Radford.

Below: Eisenhower's visit to Korea when he was President-elect reassured the public as to his intentions in this area.

liked playing hard too and having enough time to fit in his favorite pursuits of golf and bridge. Nonpolitician that he claimed to be, his grasp of many subjects was only skin deep and he relied on his personal assistant, Sherman Adams, to draw to his attention to and simplify complexities that needed mastering. Remembering the occasions when Marshall and others had called upon him for his proposed solutions to tough military problems and had been given concise replies, he himself now called for analyses of economic and diplomatic puzzles that were clearly stated on a single sheet or paper. Adams, like Bedell Smith in the same role before him, served Eisenhower with exemplary dedication. In fact he made himself indispensable. When, toward the end of Eisenhower's second term as President, in 1958, Adams was exposed by a congressional committee as having been indiscreetly associated with a New England business man who was in tax trouble, Eisenhower kept him in the job, pleading for his retention with the somewhat pathetic words, 'I need him.' But Adams was forced to resign. Even the President could not subdue public virulence.

Eisenhower was 62 when he took office; when he handed over the Presidency to John F Kennedy in January

Above: Eisenhower eats chow with men of the 15th Infantry Regiment on 4 12 1952 during his fact-finding tour of Korea.

Below: Throughout his presidency Eisenhower maintained a keen interest in army affairs.

Above: Eisenhower greets Queen Elizabeth II at MATS Terminal, National Airport on 17 10 1957.

Left: The inauguration ceremony of President Eisenhower and Vice-President Nixon for their second term of office. He won with a very comfortable majority.

1961 he was 70. His second term as President, begun in 1956, had confirmed his popularity by an even greater vote than before. This time he polled 35,590,000 votes, Adlai Stevenson 26,022,000. 'We Like Ike' had grown from a button-badge expression to a nationwide chant, and perhaps had been influenced by the sympathy the nation felt for him when, in 1955, he had suffered a heart attack and shortly after had had to have surgery for an intestinal obstruction. Then came a stroke which left him with a speech impediment from which he recovered by way of therapy. These illnesses and the periods of convalescence following them inevitably meant his absence from the White House at times of crisis – and crises in national and international affairs always abound. Without Adams, who had been called with some cynicism 'the instrument by which Dwight D Eisenhower accomplished one of the most thorough-going withdrawals from the duties of the Presidency in the history of the office' he was compelled, through the system of deployment of duties he had instituted, to become something of a rubber stamp,

Above: President Eisenhower places a wreath at the tomb of the Unknown Soldier of World War I at Arlington National Cemetery.

Below: President Ngo Dihn Diem of Viet Nam tours with Eisenhower after receiving full military honors at Washington Airport.

a benevolent constitutional monarch to whom the glamorous trappings of heroism still clung. In speeches his favorite phrases had always been 'middle of the road' and 'dynamic conservatism' and in time these phrases came to be seen to be empty of meaning. One political scientist pointed out that in the sphere of economics 'dynamic conservatism' had merely meant that there were more millionaires in the cabinet than ever before and that the President's reverance for business men had resulted less in prosperity for the nation than in prosperity for the ever-increasing number of mighty industrial conglomerates.

Eisenhower's main reverence, not un-

Above: President Eisenhower, the first SACEUR, revisits SHAPE headquarters on 3 9 1959.

Above left: Eisenhower looks on as Krushchev makes his address during his historic visit to the United States.

Left: President Eisenhower welcomes Krushchev to the United States at Andrews Air Force Base, Maryland.

Above: Eisenhower and members of the review party await the Retreat Parade to mark the Organization Day of the famed 3rd Infantry.

naturally, was for the army; and when the obsessive McCarthy, his fingers probing into alleged Communist infiltration into every walk of life, detected what he shouted about loud and long as 'subversion' in the army at Fort Monmouth, New Jersey, the President stood no more nonsense and called for an Army versus McCarthy hearing. The hearing was the hit of television in 1954. It ran for 35 days, had a bigger audience than even the Presidential elections, and revealed McCarthy and his two sleek young assistants, David Schine and Roy Cohn, as 'no more than creepy-crawlies from the jungle of Nazism.' America suddenly woke up to the fact that throughout his uncontrolled ranting and raving about Communist infiltration into government departments McCarthy had produced no evidence whatever to support his charges. He was no more than a self-interested windbag who had ruined the careers of many, an illusionist who had caught a gullible public at a sensitive moment. He was reviled by the Senate in a vote that stamped him out of the House and was subsequently ignored by the media which had elevated him briefly to notoriety; he died in obscurity in 1957.

Another worldwide sensation of Eisenhouwer's Presidency was the case of racial discrimination that reached its climax at Little Rock, Arkansas. In this he proved that he had not been in the army for 35 years for nothing; he was going to apply the rules. He enforced the law by sending troops when local authorities openly defied the federal laws, as at Little Rock; but he also admitted publicly that he did not believe 'that you can change the hearts of men with laws and decisions.' It is true that in the southern States racial integration was little more advanced after the Little Rock riots than in 1954. It was another of the problems that no amulet could charm away.

After his retirement in 1961, when he was succeeded by the charismatic John F Kennedy, Eisenhower lived for another eight years. He lived to see his chosen Vice-President, Richard Nixon, in office but happily was spared knowledge of his downfall. The Eisenhower era had begun with great hopes of economic success, international peace, scientific advancements to aid humanity and all the trappings of recovery. In that it was like all other eras. Some of those hopes had been fulfilled, many of them had been dashed to the ground. 'Middle of the road' and 'dynamic conservatism' may have been, as the critical political scientist said, meaningless phrases. Eisenhower may have been, as others have said, complacent, conformist and materialistic. But if the nation he led did not take any particularly great strides forward during his leadership, neither can it be denied its achievements. Eisenhower was not a man for all seasons: he

Above right: The coffin of Eisenhower arrives for the lying-in-state at the Capitol building, Washington.

Right: President De Gaulle salutes before the coffin of Eisenhower, whose death touched the world.

Above: Eisenhower, a crowd-pulling speaker at all public events, addresses the audience at Carlisle Barracks.

was a man for a mold in time into which he fitted exactly. The time past, he was eased by an immense popularity which he enjoyed but claimed never to have sought into another mold which fitted him less well. He was fully aware of many of the limitations of his own character and tried to avoid the effect of those limitations on a task that demanded different boundaries altogether. It is a gentle irony that it was his most outstanding quality, his devotion to duty, that led him to the Presidency. In the four score years of his life he never veered from that devotion to duty as he saw it. Possibly his view was from time to time distorted; but it was his and he held to it. He did not leave the world unhonored and unsung. He deserved both honor and praise.

INDEX

ACKNOWLEDGMENTS

Associated Press Photo, 111
Bison, 26 (top), 96–97, 102 (top and center), 110 (top and right), 119 (top)
British Official 68 (below)
Bundesarchiv 22 (below)
Fujiphotos Tokyo/Mars 21
Robert Hunt 54
Imperial War Museum 43, 55, 59, 88 (top)
Imperial War Museum/Mars 14–15, 16–17 (main pic), 35, 48 (top), 55, 62, 70 (top), 91 (top), 102–03 (below), 110 (below)
Imperial War/PPL 32–33, 42, 57, 63, 85 (top)
Keystone 52, 146–47 (all three), 157 (both)
Library of Congress 36

Mainchini Newspapers 26 (below)
Marine Corps 128 (below) 129 (top)
Military Archive and Research Services, London, 10, 12, 90 (below), 105 (top), 109 (below)
Musée de l'Armee 53
Richard Natkiel 60 (top), 81, 108–09 (top), 113 (top right)
National Archives 7, 28–29, 37, 82, 98–99 (main pic), 101, 104–05 (main pic), 105 (top right), 107 (top)
Popperfoto 45 (top two)
Sabena, print Faces 49 (top)
Signal Corps 17 (top), 20, 24
US Army 8, 9, 11, 18, 22 (top), 23, 25, 34, 38, 39, 40, 64, 65, 66, 67, 68 (top), 91 (below), 94–95, 100, 107 (below), 110 (top left), 112 (top left), 115 (both),

116–17 (all five), 118 (top), 119 (below), 120 (both), 121 (bottom), 122–23 (all six), 124–25 (all five), 126–27 (all four), 129 (below), 131, 134–35 (all three), 136, 137, 138–39 (all three), 140–41 (all four), 142–43 (all three), 145, 148–49 (all four), 150, 151, 152–53 (all three), 154–55 (all three), 156
US Army/MARS 13, 44–45 (below), 46 (top), 46–47 (below), 49 (below), 50–51, 60–61 (below), 74–75 (all three), 86, 88 (center), 88–89 (main pic), 90 (top), 114, 118 (below), 121 (top center), 132–33 (both)
USAF 105 (top left), 114 (below), 128 (top center)
USAF/MARS 70 (below), 72–73

(both), 92–93
US Archives/PPL 27
US Coast Guard 103 (top)
US Coast Guard/MARS 98 (top)
US Navy 31
US Navy/MARS 106 (below), 112–13 (below)

The author would like to thank Laurence Bradbury, the designer, Fiona Barlow, design assistant, Richard Natkiel who drew the maps, Penny Murphy, who prepared the index and Jane Laslett, the editor